PAUSE

PAUSE

everyday prayers for everyday women

betsy lowery

Revell

Grand Rapids, Michigan

© 2004 by Betsy Lowery

Published by Fleming H. Revell
a division of Baker Publishing Group
P.O. Box 6287, Grand Rapids, MI 49516-6287
www.revellbooks.com

Printed in the United States of America

Library of Congress Cataloging-in-Publication Data
Lowery, Betsy, 1960–
    Pause: everyday prayers for everyday women / Betsy Lowery.
        p.   cm.
    Includes index.
    ISBN 0-8007-5927-3 (pbk.)
    1. Christian women—Prayer-books and devotions—English. I. Title.
BV283.W6L69 2004
    242'.843—dc22   2003027479

This book is dedicated to
my mother,
a woman superlative
in generosity,
kindness, patience, gentleness,
talent, creativity, career,
knowledge, intelligence, practicality,
service, concern,
spiritual maturity, faith,
beauty, and love:

Peggy P. Criminger

In loving memory
August 24, 2002

contents

a word to the reader

Have you ever arrived for an appointment only to find that you had written the wrong time on your calendar? Have you clipped coupons during your child's ball practice or applied the finishing touches of your makeup while driving to work? Has a "Superwoman" sense of self-sufficiency sometimes kept you from depending on God? Have you ever fallen into bed exhausted and wondered as your mind and body tried to relax, *What am I really accomplishing with my life?* If your answer to any of these questions is "yes," then this book is for you.

From the home to the office to the shopping mall to the soccer sideline, God reveals opportunities for a woman to pray for positive change in herself and in the people and situations she encounters. This book may help you recognize and seize more of those opportunities.

But what *is* prayer, anyway? Is some secret formula for prayer hidden to most of us, one that would "work better" than what we have been doing if only we knew what it was? No, prayer is not a maneuver we learn to perform in a particular way, by which we can coax certain actions out of God. Rather, it is the continuing evidence of the relationship between God and a person. Not unlike conversations or letters between people, prayer can include statements, questions, expressions of joy and fear and worry, frustrated venting, tearful grieving, and the sharing of nonverbal focus on one another.

God answers prayer. It would be nice if the answers were always immediate and crystal clear. Sometimes they are. But sometimes the answers come later, during the morning drive to work, while shopping for groceries, through something heard on the radio, or (even!) in the middle of a worship service. Sometimes the answer isn't even an *answer*, as in "yes," "no," or "take that job." Sometimes the answer is, "I will show you the joy of depending on me, trusting me, and loving me in spite of your unanswered questions."

Prayers usually end with "Amen." I have not placed that word at the end of each daily prayer for two reasons: eventually it would look meaningless, and I do not want that word to end your praying if you are inclined to continue—as I hope you will be. Try using a journal along with this book to record your own praises, prayer needs, and reactions to Bible passages mentioned. You might want to do this at the start of your day, over lunch, or whenever you have your regular time of Bible study and prayer. It might even work for you to read the next day's prayer the night before, then sleep on it. You can use the topical index to find material on specific subjects, too.

Believers are instructed in the Bible to encourage one another and to comfort one another with the comfort we ourselves have received from God during particular trials (see 2 Cor. 1:4). The desire to give encouragement and comfort has motivated me to write this book more than anything else. This book's purpose is not to convince you to pray the way I pray. I have asked God, who has brought this project to completion, to bless you and to open to you new avenues of prayer and ministry.

I believe that if you invest time in this book and act on how you are prompted through it in the power of the Holy Spirit, you will learn new things about God, about the Bible, about prayer, and about yourself. I further believe that you and the people you relate to will be affected positively because of your investment in your own spiritual growth. It is my hope that this book will inspire you to pray often, honestly, at length, and about everything you encounter in life.

I urge you to pause when you experience the nudging that whispers inside you, *I need to pray.* Choose at that moment to turn off the TV, walk away from the craft project, or close the novel, and gladly answer the call to pray. It *is* a call, not just a passing thought. It is the Holy Spirit at work in you! Unseen victories you may never know about will occur every time you answer the call to pray!

May you and those you influence be blessed as you continue to grow in your faith.

january

what's new about this new year?

So if anyone is in Christ, there is a new creation; everything old has passed away; see, everything has become new!

2 CORINTHIANS 5:17

▬ January 1

God in heaven, your name is sacred. It is holy, as you are holy. To address you and refer to you, I need a distinctive name that identifies you as the one true, everlasting God of the universe! Open yourself and the pages of Scripture to me, revealing your names. Alpha and Omega! Rock. Redeemer. One name could never capture the essence of you. Master! I am proud to name as my personal authority the King of Kings and Lord of Lords! Greetings, Master! Teach me in this new year, I pray, to understand your holiness better and to respond more appropriately to it. Help me honor your holy name in the things I say and do.

▬ January 2

I believe you saved me, dear God, when I asked you to. I trust completely that I have been made new in Jesus Christ, as 2 Corinthians 5:17 says. I want to trust *all* of the Bible, even when my intellect says, "Hold on. What about the case where . . . ?" This verse claims that *everything* old has passed away and *everything* has become new. This is a big spiritual crossroads and faith challenge: accepting that regrettable events, relationships, and mistakes really have "passed away." I want to believe that; help me believe it! I want the words of that Scripture verse and many others to move off the page and become true in my life this year.

▬ January 3

Father, I would rather not pray at all than to tell you lies, so help me pray honestly and sincerely. Draw me into your presence eagerly and boldly but never without humility. Your ways are above mine, dear God. May your will, not mine, be done. Give me more discipline in prayer. Develop in my life a maturing prayer ministry and a greater knowledge of the one to whom I address my prayers. Reveal my sins to me so I can confess them and be made righteous again in your sight—then my prayers will be powerful and effective (James 5:16).

■ January 4

Holy Spirit, teach me what praying really is so that when I spend time doing what I think is praying, I'm not just thinking out loud or wishing. Teach me to pray according to the truth of Scripture, not according to the values of secular culture and a self-centered worldview. Help me, God, to conform to your image, knowing that when I do so I become the very best and most eternity-fit "me" possible. This year please help me keep my priorities balanced so that I can prepare for heaven and be useful on earth at the same time.

■ January 5

Father God, *all* the help that's available from you—that's what I want and need! Please pour it over me. Open my mind to the truth. Give my faith more practical application to everyday situations. Improve my habits and hold me back from making stupid mistakes. This life is short, and I don't want it to keep slipping away without my knowing what its purpose has been or will be. I have goals: to be more thankful, content, patient, loving, and verbally appreciative; to be less critical; to accomplish important things. Thank you for caring about my goals. Help me bring my goals into line with yours.

▰ January 6

The writer of Ecclesiastes lamented, "There is nothing new under the sun" (1:9). History does seem to repeat itself. We live but don't learn. We raise deep questions, choose faulty answers, then reject those answers for "better" ones that are just as faulty. Thank you, Lord, for making your wisdom available in Scripture; lead me not only to consult it but also to practice it. Lord, some view the Bible as a book of myths or a crutch for the weak. Your Word is neither! Draw me to it. As I read with a desire to be changed, open my eyes to the Bible's answers for the issues I face. Draw me to you, my Answer.

▰ January 7

Psalm 16:2 reads, "You are my Lord; I have no good apart from you." These words reveal a relationship that goes beyond whatever "good" the writer had or hoped to have. Lord, I believe that my praying will be more substantial and satisfying if it is relationship-oriented rather than outcome-oriented. The Bible says you, like a loving parent, gladly give us good gifts (Matt. 7:11), but gifts mean less when we ignore the giver. I never want to give you the impression that I would prefer to have you drop the gift on the doorstep and then leave! I'm sorry if I have behaved that way.

▰ January 8

Words are powerful, Lord, and I want to use that power more constructively. Make me aware of the careless words that come out of my mouth with greater frequency than I realize: *stupid, jerk, idiot.* And sometimes worse words rush out of my mouth (or at least through my mind) to inflict hurt. I want my words to be more careful and kinder, reflective of your heart, Lord. If I am to be your ambassador, I will have to speak wisely. Give me Spirit-led words of life and power that build people up and claim positive outcomes. Show me daily how to support and encourage the people with whom I live and work with wise, well-chosen words.

▬ January 9

Father, I want things to feel new and exciting when that's possible, but I don't want to wake up each morning feeling so new that I have no idea who I was yesterday! I want to get up today and step widely away from yesterday's imperfect assumptions. Help me to feel the way I feel when I walk out of a theater after having been completely absorbed in a movie: I step back into my same life at the same point where I stepped out of it, but I have a strangely fresher attitude. Please give me that kind of freshness. I need it badly!

▬ January 10

Lord Jesus, teach me to pray. The disciples said that, and Luke's account indicates that the request was interpreted, "Demonstrate for us how we should pray." I want to learn from the prayer you spoke then, Lord. But I also want you to teach me *to* pray. Apparently praying is not the most natural impulse, or I would not find so many hours filled with everything *but* prayer. Teach me to assign a certain portion of my day to prayer and to feel very out of sorts if I miss that appointment. Teach me to pray with more knowledge of your ways. Teach me to pray powerfully. Teach me not to ask "wrongly" (James 4:3).

▰ January 11

Lord, what if I discovered the following note?

Dear Mom,

Hi! I drew this picture 4 U 2day. I'm sorry I knocked that bag off the table and broke the jar of pickles. I hope U R not too mad at me. Thank you for helping me clean it up. I was hoping Rachel could come over on Saturday. Please? I luv U!

Samantha

I expect I would be touched by the picture, understanding about the "sorry," and reasonably open to the request. But how often have I sent notes to you with no greeting, no expression of affection, no confession of sin, no thanks? Just "Here's what I want right now, Lord. Pleeeze? Okay, gotta go!" Forgive me for treating you that way. It is selfish and inappropriate. Teach me to pray with more maturity than that.

▰ January 12

Dear heavenly Father, I'm so glad to know that because I am your child, I don't have to start from scratch with you each time I pray. But do not let me abuse that familiarity, forgetting even to say "hello" in my haste to call to your attention my list of needs. You know better than I do what business is most important for this moment we are spending together. You know what events will affect my life throughout this day. Prepare me right now, I pray, for those events. Finally, Lord, please forgive me for spending more time trading "prayer requests" than actually praying.

▰ January 13

Show me more about what prayer is, most holy God! I cherish the time I spend bowed before you, but I need more. I long to give you time in my all-day-long life. I want you to have priority in my thinking. I need a constant connection with you. Show me how I can understand your mind and be sure of what you are telling me. I want fewer times of second-guessing what is and is not your leading. Teach me to know your voice—*really* know it—and to distinguish it clearly from my own thoughts, from the marketing devices of secular culture, and from the cleverly disguised enticements of Satan.

▰ January 14

Father, make me a more generous person, more inclined to share than to hoard. Jesus held nothing back; may I aspire to follow his example. And, Father, when I observe a friend or family member *not* being generous, let me carefully consider whether it is appropriate to suggest, "You ought to be less selfish." Make me a good example in my actions on any matter about which I propose to advise someone else. And on the subject of generosity, thank you for my friends' generosity with their belongings. If there are items in my home or car that I've borrowed and need to return, please help me do that this week.

▰ January 15

Thank you, God, for every basic blessing staring me in the face today: the food I eat, the water I drink, the clothes I wear, the vehicle I drive, the place I live, the parents who gave me life, the health I enjoy, and the family and friends you have given me. Help me understand how blessed I am to have these things! And the list doesn't stop there. You have heaped other benefits on me: travel, education, work, creativity, and the opportunity to enjoy art and literature. Sometimes I focus so much on how much more I hope to have someday that I don't appreciate what I have right now. Forgive me, please, and accept my gratitude.

▬ January 16

Please give me greater fortitude and drive, Lord. This life certainly requires plenty of both for coping with work, family, large and small crises, emotional ups and downs, and the endless mundane tasks of meal preparation, household paperwork, laundry, dusting, and on and on! I need my internal radar fixed on the truth that nothing—nothing bad, good, indifferent, stupid, boring, frustrating, or confusing—*nothing* can separate me from you and your unchanging love for me. I need to recall that fact more and more as time passes. God, make your love so plain and so amazing to me that I cannot help but tell about it.

▬ January 17

Thank you, Father and Guide, for these encouraging words: "The light of the eyes rejoices the heart, and good news refreshes the body" (Prov. 15:30). You know so well how much I need light in my eyes and something—anything!—to refresh my body! Super-paced living means some mornings I can barely get my eyes *open*, much less have a bright and happy light in them. And is there any good news on TV that refreshes my body? Almost never. O my Helper! Remind me that "Jesus lives!" is the *real* news of the day, not which multibillion-dollar corporation failed and how many lives were claimed by accident and crime.

▬ January 18

Lord, I want good news to refresh my body. I also want good skin care, hair care, and exercise to make my body healthy and attractive. I am envious of the woman who appears to have perfect hair, skin, and teeth—and a model's figure wrapped in expensive clothing. Yes, I would like to be a really fine-looking temple for you, Lord! But you know that it is mostly ego and a competitive desire for the incidental roving male eye that drives my need to look good. Help me accept that my body is temporary, mortal, and incapable of perfection. And when I feel that jealous twinge over a better-looking woman, prompt me to pray that her life will be as beautiful as her appearance.

▬ January 19

Father, what do you suppose I could accomplish as a woman with the body of age twenty, the energy of age three, the savvy of age fifty-four, the daring of age fifteen, and the wisdom of old age? Add in the blamelessness of a newborn, and would I not be amazingly capable? But would I invest those assets in virtuous goals of lasting value? Or would I grow terribly prideful and power-hungry? You have given some of these good traits at different stages of life. Some decrease as others increase. So I ask you to sustain my body, renew my energy, hone my savvy, surface my daring, increase my wisdom, and lead me in right paths, to the end that I would honor you and give you the glory for anything I accomplish.

▪ January 20

Lord, I admit that prayer for government leaders usually falls in third place, after discussion of their actions and criticism of their motives. Forgive me for that. Help the men and women who serve in government, for only with honorable and courageous individuals will we assemble a strong government. Guide these people not just in their government service, but in health, family life, and each big and small personal need. This is a huge, sweeping prayer. But you are a huge, sweeping God! I believe that you will move unmistakably in the lives of these many people because your child has asked you to do that.

▪ January 21

Thank you, God, for hearing my prayers because you love me. Make my praying more than a daily supervisor/supervisee check-in meeting. Make my praying sincere and reverent whether it is worded formally in a church setting or worded conversationally in a minivan or at the kitchen sink. Be my Lord as well as my God. Show me if I have been praying incorrectly, trying to persuade you to adjust your eternal plan to my temporary and often poorly thought-out wishes. I quote Galatians 2:20, "I am crucified with Christ," with good intentions, but in any given twenty-four-hour period, I seem to be a rather spry corpse, trying to keep living for myself.

▪ January 22

Father, you called your people, through Ezekiel, to get a new heart and a new spirit. Sometimes my heart and spirit seem badly in need of replacement. I need a new attitude and fresh motivation every day. I want to be righteous in your sight. These things do not come easily. Sometimes the path seems very clear; and at other times it's lost in a muddle of fatigue and confusion. Make the truth plain to me and the path straight for my feet. I take a dangerous course when I leave prayer out of a three- to ten-day stretch of "ordinary" days! Call me out of that complacent mode. I need to seek you in prayer every day.

▬ January 23

Help me, Lord, when the time I need to spend on housework and family is in conflict with the time I need to reserve for prayer and Bible study without distraction. It should not be one "versus" the other! If I neglect my spiritual needs, I will not treat my family well. But if I ignore my husband and children when they really need me in order to go off somewhere and "be spiritual," they will resent that. Part of my growth in faith is in merging the two responsibilities. Help me involve my family in my quest for spiritual growth so I can teach them, learn from them, and have them call me to account on certain things when I am not acting in accordance with the spiritual goals they know I have adopted.

▬ January 24

Savior, you already know about the work conflict, the friend with cancer, the relative looking for a job, and the personal struggle over a bothersome issue or destructive habit. Besides asking for your power in these situations, reveal to me how I can rid myself of the stuff that doesn't belong in the life of one who calls you Master. I mean both the Ten Commandments kind of sins and other, more subtle things. Breaking a promise to take my child to the park because something "more important" came up. Using the power of my speech to "discuss" the annoying habits of someone in the community. Teach me to be less like that and more like you.

▬ January 25

Lord, your servant Paul wrote, "We are slaves not under the old written code but in the new life of the Spirit" (Rom. 7:6). By your power, make those words live in us. Lord, you have given commandments to us for our protection and benefit, but you also have given us the freedom of not being stressed out over excessive numbers of picky requirements that are supposed to "prove" our allegiance. You want our hearts, not just our activities! Let us not devalue your grace by behaving as if anything we do earns it initially or maintains it. Grace is undeserved by definition. Thank you for that amazing gift!

▬ January 26

Sometimes my first coherent thought of the day is, *I'm not particularly excited about this day's agenda.* When that happens, Father, move my lips to call on the power of your name for the task of moving my under-rested body out of bed to go wake the children for school, take a shower, and produce a breakfast. Colossians 3:23 admonishes believers to do whatever is on the agenda as if in direct service to you rather than to a human authority figure (such as my self-driven self!). I have to be honest—even thinking of that Bible verse doesn't always improve my energy level. I repeat: *Help me!*

▬ January 27

Lord, I don't like it when any old song I've heard playing over a store's sound system keeps running through my mind. They can have such inconsequential and often immoral concepts, yet I'm repeating them in my head and giving them a foothold in my brain. Make me aware of what I am hearing by accident and by choice. Thank you for the times when I've awakened to discover that a sacred song has been playing in my head before I've become conscious of it. I love that, because it proves I've been exposing my ears and thoughts to songs of truth and strength. How I spend my thoughts is an offering to you. Be Lord over what I listen to and therefore think about!

■ January 28

Thank you, God, for recorded music that helps me praise you and memorize important points of Scripture. Please bless each musician and technician who has had a part in creating the Christian recordings that are valuable and helpful to me. Some of those people may be embarking on new lines of work or may be struggling now, feeling very different about faith matters than they did when working on the songs I still listen to. Certainly they all have daily challenges and "stuff and junk" in their lives just as I do. I owe them a debt of gratitude, and praying for them is the only way I can pay that debt.

■ January 29

Lord, when I see buses leaving school property for a field trip, call me to pray at that moment for the safety of the students, teachers, chaperones, and drivers; for your name to be honored in their conversations; and for those who have hurts and troubles to be helped during that trip by someone who makes a positive remark or simply listens. Make me faithful to pray often for safety and for Christian influence in our schools. Prayer of that type is a duty, and so what if "duty" is unpopular jargon even in the church? Make me faithful to perform duties gladly from a heart that is attentive to your will.

▰ January 30

Father God, I believe with all my heart that you will work because I ask you to and that my prayer will make a difference in someone's life. That is why I often pray for the people who walk or work along the side of the road. If I do not pray, I am dismissing precious souls whom you have created as if they were part of inconsequential scenery. Population is growing staggeringly, but the numbers are still finite. You are infinite! You see each person. Crowdedness makes people feel insignificant and anonymous, but your Word proclaims that people are of great value to you. We love to think of that as it applies to ourselves. Help us remember that it applies to everyone.

▰ January 31

The Ten Commandments were given through Moses. The priests and prophets relayed your continuing commands for the nation of Israel. Jesus made the commandments more personal, requiring purity of thought as well as action. Wait! We don't want to be *commanded*, Lord! We want to be free, independent, in control of "our" lives. But that's just it. Whose life is it, anyway? If we are operating in the Spirit, not in the flesh, we will learn to love your commandments. I want to follow your commandments, Lord God, and I want to love them. I long to see your commandments move people to demonstrate courtesy, courage, moral conviction, and even heroism. If anything new is needed under the sun this year, this is it.

february

let us count the ways

God is love.

1 JOHN 4:16

▰ February 1

Heavenly Father, the Bible declares "God is love," and its pages hold many proofs and illustrations of that truth. For example, Romans 5:8 declares, "But God proves his love for us in that while we still were sinners Christ died for us." Thank you, God, for the gift that expresses your love so fully: forgiveness. No matter how bad things are, how horribly I mess up, how tangled and marred life might become, your forgiveness is available to me. If I did not have this knowledge, how frightened, worried, and insecure I would be! Thank you that I can stand clean before you with the righteousness and perfection of Jesus covering my sinful nature and each specific failing.

▰ February 2

Thank you, God, for the practical gift of your love that is the book of Proverbs. Its pages are full of incisive truths about our human nature and how we can best deal with it as we try to please you and to get along with others. Many times I have seen Proverbs 15:1 lived out: a soft answer turns anger away. Too often I've seen vicious verbal exchanges occur when this proverb is forgotten. O Lord, how easy I find it to lash out when accosted with hostile words, especially when I feel I've been treated badly. Next time, flash this proverb in my mind before angry words escape. Let me live in the victory of seeing wisdom and patience rule over rashness and pride.

▰ February 3

Thank you, kind Father, for the friends who have blessed my life. Thank you for their love, support, intelligence, humor, talents, companionship, humility, and dependability. Some friends have moved far beyond my reach by now, out of sight. Out of remembrance, almost. Names of people who played a significant role early in my life might escape me now, but I'm thankful for what I gained from knowing each one. I am thankful for the wonderful and caring individuals who enrich my life right now. Bless all of them, Lord, old friends as well as new. And make me a more attentive and helpful friend.

■ February 4

On this winter day, loving Lord, I need warmth and comfort in spirit as well as in body. Your many gifts of love are cause for a warm feeling of thankfulness and of being cared for! Today I thank you especially for the gift of answered prayer. Knowing that you hear and answer your children's prayers is so important! I'd like someday to see a written list of all my prayers along with how you answered them. Why a list? I suppose because it would be such a great testimony to how you love by saying yes to some things and no to things that you know would not be beneficial or that simply are not in your plan.

■ February 5

Father God, one of the ways your love is demonstrated is the fact that you are true to your Word. When the Bible speaks of your love, I can believe what I read. When it speaks of your faithfulness, I can depend on that! When it speaks of you abiding in me and I in you (John 15:4), I can testify personally that my heart and your heart have become intertwined in that abiding process. I am convinced that when certain things grieve me, my grief is your grief. It is a matter of unity, Lord. Your Word promises me that this oneness occurs between you and those who choose your lordship in their lives. Thank you for being true to your Word!

▰ February 6

What a fascinatingly beautiful gift you give us each day in the sky that paints a canopy over the earth, most awesome God! Let every morning be a reminder that your mighty hands still turn the earth, bringing day and night consistently and miraculously. Thank you for the ever-changing appearances of the sky. What beauty it holds for my eyes to drink in! Thank you for the fiery brilliance of sunset and the twinkling allure of evening stars. My words could never do justice to your magnificent artistry, Lord. Still, I must try to express my gratitude. If the skies I have seen are a sample, then how beautiful heaven must be!

▰ February 7

Thank you, Father, for smiles on the faces of children. Children's natural enthusiasm is surely of your making! Protect the children, O God! Hear the cries of the hungry, the neglected, and the abused. Intervene where the child is too young and innocent to know to cry for help. Help where only you can help, and move people to help when and how they can. Forgive me for when I've been too busy to see children smile or to see their need for a smile from me. Thank you for those who faithfully work with children; reward them in many ways. When they receive smiles from the children they care for, may they recognize those smiles as gifts from you.

▰ February 8

Thank you, Lord, for sights in the natural world that bring pleasure to my eyes and laughter to my soul. Thank you for the whimsical enjoyment of seeing a troop of dry leaves scurrying with purpose as the wind gives them life. Dead leaves dancing, jumping, hopping! When I see such sights I often think, *This is such a vivid expression of what God is like!* Simple, appealing, captivating sights—they minister to my soul, Lord, even when my soul gets quite weary. Thank you for the dead leaves dancing and for bringing life and energy to things, situations, and relationships that have been dead and stale.

▀ February 9

Dear God and giver of all life, I thank you today for the miracle of birth. Birth is most assuredly a miracle, Lord, as life emerges against so many odds! Bless those experiencing this miracle in their families. Grant joy, physical assistance, and rest. Send angels and ministers of mercy to those who have mixed or negative emotions about a birth and the circumstances surrounding it. Wrap your arms of comfort around all who long to have children but still are waiting or have given up. Help them when insensitive and unkind things are said to or around them. And, Lord, strengthen those who deal daily with difficult physical challenges present since birth.

▀ February 10

What a beautiful expression of your love is in the book of John, chapter 17, dear Lord—the account of your prayer for me! In the person of Jesus, you expressed a prayer at a real moment in time, with a real human voice, *for me.* You prayed for those who would later come to believe in you. Thank you, precious Lord, for praying for me and allowing me to read the words you spoke on my behalf! Thank you also that this example of collective praying validates the collective praying I sometimes do for "medical professionals," "truck drivers," "missionaries," "police officers," "parents," "church leaders," and so forth. You know the people in these groups, and you know the needs of each person.

■ February 11

One of your most precious gifts of love is the wise guidance of spiritual mentors, dear Father. Thank you for the leadership and inspiration of pastors, teachers, and wise, caring friends. Help us learn from these people while being careful that what they advise is not contrary to your revealed will. Bless and strengthen the persons you have called into ministry, paid or volunteer. Keep them blameless, pure, and in tune with your Spirit so that their counsel will be correct. And, Lord, make me attentive to the opportunities I can seize to develop my own maturity to the point where I can step into a mentor role when someone needs that from me.

■ February 12

Thank you, God, not only for the mentors we have sought out, but also for those in authority and others we did not seek out or willingly place ourselves under. You knew, Lord, our need to be under authority. You knew we needed the care of parents when we were helpless children. You have provided instruction and wisdom for us through teachers, in church and in school. You have given us workplace supervisors, law enforcement workers, and government leaders for our benefit. Thank you for establishing authority and order. Make us quicker to support and pray for our authorities than to criticize and resent them. Thank you for the servant leadership Jesus modeled. Make me a wise leader to those over whom I have authority.

■ February 13

Thank you, heavenly Father and miraculous Creator, for the singing of birds that punctuates my experience of the natural world.

You have an important message for me in that the birds continue chirping no matter what is going on in the world! It is a reminder of your control over all things and a proclamation that creation has an ongoing beauty unmarred by the ugliness that is in the human story. Scripture tells us that the birds are valuable to you, Lord—not one of them falling from its nest goes unnoticed by you. You care for them; you care for me even more (Matt. 10:29–31).

▰ February 14

Lord Jesus, you announced to your followers, "I give you a new commandment, that you love one another" (John 13:34). I thank you today for the people I love and for the people who love me. Thank you that you have allowed us to know the joy of loving and being loved on so many levels and in so many contexts. When we experience the thrill of attraction, the hurt of rejection, the pain of tough love, and the numerous challenges of being committed to marriages and other long-term relationships, give us wisdom. When others come to us for advice, speak your counsel through us. For all who are frustrated or sorrowful about love matters today, I ask a special measure of your comfort and guidance.

▰ February 15

Heavenly Father, steer me away from thinking that you did not plan ahead for how the world's population would grow when you directed the first people to "be fruitful and multiply." Steer me and others away from the idea that any one individual could not matter much to you because there are so many people. Our feeble minds simply hinder us from grasping the infinity of your wisdom and your love! If we ever begin to doubt your interest in each individual's welfare, then we have doubted Scripture and your character as revealed there. Forgive us for doubting. Increase our faith! Increase our passion to tell others, "God cares about you."

■ February 16

Although it's not always a happy, pleasant-feeling gift, wise Father, your gift of conscience is a good gift and one I am thankful for. Without conscience, what a fearsome life this would be. Without the ability to engage in honest self-evaluation, how much blinder and more misguided people would be. Enable me more often to see myself—and *hear* myself—as others do. Give me more insight about myself and more moments of productive self-appraisal, but keep me from going to the extreme of belittling myself and losing confidence. Sharpen my conscience, dear Lord. Repair it where it is weak and compromised. I need your guidance and wisdom to understand and use my conscience as you intend.

■ February 17

The human body is a miracle of unequaled measure in your creation, God. Athletics and dance show such beauty of motion and trained ability. Even everyday activities employ the simple grace of walking, running, stretching, and bending. The phenomenal tools we call hands can work, play, and create. Inside us amazing processes are carried out by systems and organs. Thank you for all the parts of my body that work correctly. Thank you for the body's capacity to heal from injury and surgery. My body is a gift from your loving hand; help me care for it well.

▬ February 18

Thank you, God, for the comfort I've received from a caring person when I've been annoyed or unglued. Thank you equally for when I've been able to help a friend, even if I said little more than, "I know. *Believe me,* I know!" Thank you, Lord, for not leaving your people comfortless. Lord, I don't rejoice in suffering and tragedy with a false sense of piety, saying, "This is actually wonderful because it will lead to blessing and growth." But I do thank you that some type of blessing almost always occurs where sorrow has created a void. Thank you, too, for the little silver linings I experience in the midst of day-to-day trials.

▬ February 19

Our children are such a treasure, Lord—a gift from you, a heritage and a reward (Ps. 127:3). Remind me of this more often so I don't take my children for granted, forgetting how passionately I anticipated their arrival and attended to their every move and need when they were so small. True, we find more stubborn independence and defiance to deal with in them when they are older, but we also find great amusement at their silly antics and great pride in their accomplishments. Thank you for the great friendship that can be found with sons and daughters and for the caregiving by children for aged parents. Thank you for loving us through the gift of our children.

▬ February 20

One of the greatest evidences of your unfailing love, Lord God, is the fact that you keep right on loving me in spite of how I often ignore you! When my life is filled with smooth sailing, I am lulled into a state of acceptance of your love, and I forget to offer thanks to you daily for it. I even begin to think I have earned those calm waters by my own efforts! I am not proud of how I have ignored you, Lord. I am ashamed. I love you! I thank you for the many ways you demonstrate your love to me even when I do not respond.

▬ February 21

Lord, many days in a row I behave like a self-made Superwoman, confident that I have things figured out and under control. I ready myself for a busy day, grab the car keys, and drive out into who knows what kind of potential physical and spiritual peril, never having stopped long enough to ask you for your protection and guidance, much less to thank you, praise you, confess my sins, or pray for my family members' well-being. None of my high-gear projects would amount to a grain of sand if you were not sustaining me right down to the next heartbeat! Help me recognize my dependence on you and my responsibility to verbalize that dependence as I pray for myself and others.

▬ February 22

Here's something amazing: I *know* how it feels to provide, provide, provide and have that provision go completely unnoticed and unappreciated. Yet I act the very same way with you, dear Father! I often spend my valuable time returning all manner of household objects to their rightful places—toys, clothing, TV remotes, games, extra toilet paper rolls—leaving the house noticeably neater and cleaner, knowing that the difference should be so glaringly obvious to the rest of the family that they instantly verbalize their awe and appreciation. When the family then waltzes by in a state of complete ungrateful acceptance, I know how you feel when I take your precious love as if it is my due. Forgive me, please.

▬ February 23

Thank you, God, for the "daily bread" you provide. Help me to look at my daily diet and understand that it is a critical, essential provision straight from your hand, not something I have obtained by any cleverness of my own. Lord, some have too little to eat; others have too much. You are distressed that food is not distributed adequately to all who need it. Guide me to do more than I have been doing to support hunger relief. Guide me, when food is readily available, to consume appropriate amounts in healthy varieties. In eating, as in all things, you are my Lord and my leader.

▬ February 24

I am grateful to you, loving Lord, for the many extra comforts you have sent my way on top of the basic necessities you provide. As an attentive loved one gives extra touches of affection along with what is expected, you bring uncounted pleasures to my experience in the form of music, beloved reading material, favorite foods, hot tea shared with a friend, the affection of a pet, the beauty of a patchwork quilt, and the joy of making patterns in the dirt with my toes! Open my eyes and heart to the beauty of simple pleasures, Lord! They are everywhere, every day, and I don't want to miss a single one of them.

▬ February 25

Precious God, I am encouraged almost every day of my life by simple kindnesses extended by people around me. I thank you for allowing me to be blessed by people who choose to extend courtesy and thoughtful helpfulness to those around them. Moreover, my life has been touched, both directly and indirectly, by the not-so-simple kindnesses of extraordinary people—a lifeguard or police officer whose courage has achieved something brief and dramatic or a benefactor who has built an institution slowly by dedication and perseverance. Thank you for extending your love to me through people whose hearts reflect the character of their Maker.

▉ February 26

Thank you for mild winter days that preview the coming of spring. My thoughts turn to warm-weather vacationing, and often that brings to mind a visit to the beach. The ocean is something it seems we never tire of experiencing with all five senses. Thank you for this beautiful gift, loving God! The waves are constant and powerful; the sand is a never-boring playground. Walking at the edge of the surf can be one of the most calming and at the same time inspiring experiences we ever know. If I visit the coast this year, Lord, cause me to marvel at its vast beauty. Let me kneel in the sand not only to play, but to pray.

▉ February 27

Winter winds are blowing, Lord, cold and ruthless. But they remind me of what is said regarding the Holy Spirit in John 3:8: "The wind blows where it chooses, and you hear the sound of it, but you do not know where it comes from or where it goes." The beauty of the invisible wind is seen when a flag cascades, a sail fills, or a colorful kite soars. Send your Spirit the same way to cause beauty in our needy lives. We need the beauty of growth, accomplishment, ministry, and redemption. Lord, the wind can create havoc as well as beauty. I long to see that the wind of your Spirit has created havoc with Satan's plans.

▬ February 28

Thank you, God, for the Bible's powerfully worded assurances of your unfailing love for me! The apostle Paul wrote that "neither death, nor life, nor angels, nor rulers, nor things present, nor things to come, nor powers, nor height, nor depth, nor anything else in all creation, will be able to separate us from the love of God in Christ Jesus our Lord" (Rom. 8:38–39). I am so uplifted to know that no sin, accident, crime, opposition, anger, mistake, spoken word, indifference, arrogance, achievement, pride, doubt, or despair, and not even Satan himself, can dissolve the bond of love between you and me. Thank you, God, for your unfailing love—a love that I do not deserve and that is greater than any measure known to the human mind!

▬ February 29

Call me, Lord, to look upon this uncommon calendar date as an opportunity for the unusual, and remind me that *every* day is unique and rare no matter what number is assigned to it. After counting some of the ways you demonstrate your great love for us, I find it good also to look at some of the things you do for those who love you: you deliver them, protect them, answer them, rescue them, honor them, satisfy them, and save them (Ps. 91:14–16)! Who wouldn't want to love a God who does all of that? I am so thankful for my experience of your love. It started with forgiveness. It has grown into so much more. It will last eternally.

march

left, right, left, right . . .

Forgetting what lies behind and straining forward to what lies ahead, I press on toward the goal for the prize of the heavenly call of God in Christ Jesus.

PHILIPPIANS 3:13–14

because the day
has come

I notice on the coldest mornings,
    with or without sun,
The little birds attend to life
    because the day has come.
Engagingly they choose a perch
    or hop about the grounds,
And, scorning winter's cruelty,
    chirp bright and happy sounds.

I notice on a bitter morning,
    bitter as I see,
The birds make song regardless
    and they take no thought of me;
Unless my God has told them
    that my soul has things to mend,
And hope is what they're crying out—
    if I will tune it in.

Oh give me, God, on any morning,
    more of what I find
Remarkable in these small ones
    you've carefully designed:
Simplicity and buoyancy,
    and, more than anything,
The want—or, at the very least,
    the willingness—to sing.

▰ March 1

Spiritual Commander-in-Chief, your servant Paul spoke of "straining forward" and "pressing on." I desire to follow his example, but sometimes I feel that my life is status quo in spite of all I try to do to make it otherwise. So much of my time each day is spent maintaining and handling responsibilities set in motion by my past choices. I feel as if I am treading water, making no great progress. Encourage me, Lord! Remind me that progress is usually too gradual to detect daily.

▰ March 2

Guide me today, Lord, not to run aimlessly (1 Cor. 9:26), frantically and erratically, hassled and haggard, nor to plant myself stubbornly with a pout and folded arms. Guide me, instead, to go wherever it is you want me to go this day at the pace that is right for my state of mind, body, and spirit. If I need to hurry up or be energized, you can make that happen. If I need to slow down, tell me so, then reveal to me which agenda items are disposable. Guide my words so that whatever I say today will not be derogatory or idly unimportant. Keep my eyes on you, Lord.

▰ March 3

Father, you designed us to need work, leisure, and relationships and some measure of routine in which to manage it all. If I had no task, even one as basic as obtaining the first meal of the day, I would find it difficult sometimes to get out of bed and be productive. Guide me to see the benefit of a routine that is helpful but not inflexible. Keep me on track, even when I must make my forward progress slowly. Move me to a disciplined practice of faith so that laziness, complacency, boredom, restless philosophizing, and self-pity don't have a chance to move in and set up shop.

▬ March 4

As I listen to various calls for Christians to "do all they can" to reach others and better the world, give me a responsive heart and the will to carry out helpful actions, dear Lord! Help me to approach my response with the understanding that serving you daily does not mean killing myself with overactivity and continually holding myself up to unrealistic expectations. Focus my goals and my thinking more on quality than on quantity! Remind me, too, that there is no other person to whose life I must "measure up." You have a unique calling for me, and it will not mirror anyone else's calling.

▬ March 5

Lord, when I feel I must do *x* task *today* because time is so scarce, help me balance that sense of urgency with common sense. It's a fact that I need more rest now than I did when I was younger. It doesn't have to be more hours spent sleeping. As a child, even something as active as riding my bicycle may have been restful. Rest takes many forms. A change of scenery is often the real need. Jesus withdrew from his heavy ministry load periodically. Give me wisdom regarding the amounts of activity and rest in my schedule. Open my eyes to new avenues of rest.

▬ March 6

Father God, my praying has fallen into a pattern of asking for your help "to get through this day." When my words reveal that

I am in a defensive, survival mode, open my prayer vocabulary to capture the abundant and victorious living you desire for me! Make my requests of you bolder and more imaginative. Expand them to focus on broader concerns than just my own dreams of pleasure, love, and accomplishment. Help me to dig my heels into a prayer ministry that touches things I never thought of praying about before. Reveal your will to me as I pray; use this time to do miraculous things through my availability.

▬ March 7

Father, I know I can depend on you. Can you depend on me? Make me fit for your kingdom. I don't want to be found looking back wistfully toward a freedom or carefree time I may have thought I had earlier in life. Nor do I want to be found looking into space blankly while the baseball, as it were, comes right toward me and I totally miss making the play. It's a hard calling, Lord, but I long to be on the job for you. I will be glad, eternally glad, if I am found faithful in service to you during these brief mortal years. Strengthen me! Encourage me! Find me faithful!

▬ March 8

Remind me, precious Lord, that in your army I do not march unprotected but am wearing armor that you have provided (Eph. 6:11–18) fitted over the clothing that is your righteousness (Ps. 132:9). That's some uniform! Make me more aware of it as I attire my physical body in dresses or blue jeans. By your Spirit, also remind me that I serve a Commander who is the King of Kings and Lord of Lords. It's easy to think of that only in church, but everywhere else is where I need to think of it most!

▰ March 9

Father, my heart's desire is to serve you with joy and with confidence that my heart and my actions are pleasing to you. I *know* that my life does not go unnoticed by you even for a single minute. So help me to know that nothing sinful I do or think about doing is hidden from you. No need I experience is unseen by your shepherding eye. Help me to trust you as a wise parent rather than fear you as a stalking overseer. Help me with minute-to-minute thoughts and choices so that the long-term tracks I leave will show evidence of faithfulness, righteousness, and joy.

▰ March 10

"Happy are those who trust in the LORD" (Prov. 16:20). What a temptation to test this verse for reliability! I might suspect it is only "partly true" if I hold it up against real-life examples of unhappy Christians. It might be misused as a weapon by an insensitive do-gooder who quotes it to a grieving or cynical person. Enable my inquisitive nature to treat this and all portions of Scripture with reverence and faith, dear Lord, no matter how I might *feel* about my limited understanding of its application in thousands of cases. Give me faith to hold to your Word as truth even when I fail to understand my present relationship to that truth.

▰ March 11

God, examine my heart and make it purer. I believe you can do this; I believe you are doing this already. Purify my praying, too! Cleanse me of all my known and unknown sins. As for my needs and requests, you know already what is written on my current scrap-paper prayer list. You know I crave the same guidance, fulfilled dreams, and removal of worldwide suffering that I requested yesterday. Lord, you are God! Oh, how numbly I treat that fact most of the time. Right now renew my yearning to just *know you* and to actively anticipate being with you someday soon in a setting that exceeds my wildest expectations.

▰ March 12

Teach me, Lord, how to not worry! Worrying cannot add even a single hour to my lifetime (Luke 12:25). Teach me to trust, to be faithful and available to you, to plan, and to dream, all without adding the unhelpful ingredient of worry. You have promised to attend to my needs in addition to bringing your kingdom into my life when I seek it above all else (Luke 12:30–31). Draw my attention to your kingdom today. Lead me to resources that will equip me to be a faithful Christian, citizen, friend, wife, and mother—then tell me again that it's okay for me to forsake worry and entrust my loved ones and all other things to you.

▰ March 13

Father God, just as I am reluctant to leave my children in the care of someone I don't know well, I feel uncertain about trusting you when I feel my knowledge of you is sketchy. Increase my knowledge as I invest time in prayer and in searching the Scriptures, having asked the Holy Spirit to teach me as I read. When I am tempted to question your will and your handling of all the big issues people are facing on this earth, lead me to seek more knowledge of you so I will be ready to trust you more.

▬ March 14

Lord Jesus, when my energy is dwindling and my daily motivation for work, housework, and personal accomplishment is plummeting, sustain me, I pray. Remind me that the times of large joy and the times of peaceful satisfaction come in waves. Remind me that feelings of joy and well-being are most recognizable against the backdrop of struggle. Allow me the honesty and humility to lean on a trusted friend who is in a stage of energy when I am in a stage of blah or simply to share frustration with that friend when we both are in a stage of blah.

▬ March 15

Dear Lord, when a situation seems headed hopelessly downhill, I will keep praying for miraculous change, knowing that all things are possible with you. Call me to pray faithfully regardless of what "results" I think I am seeing or not seeing from your hand! Give me wisdom and patience when it is apparent that a desired change will take time. I know this: Praying for outlandish things I have no sensible expectation of seeing in my own lifetime is one of the most exciting things I ever do. Guide my praying so that it falls within your wonderful, mysterious will!

▬ March 16

Loving and all-encompassing God, help me focus less on my "performance" in this life and more on whom I follow and serve! Daniel 6:26–27 reads, "For he is the living God, enduring forever. His kingdom shall never be destroyed, and his dominion has no end. He delivers and rescues, he works signs and wonders in heaven and on earth." Most days I just don't grasp these things in a state of victorious faith. Most days my focus is on this present earth with all its troubles and on my own life. Open my thinking and my small talk to the immensity of your existence and your greatness!

■ March 17

Father, I am very keen on making the most of "my" time. I like having a book or an electronic game in hand at the ballpark or even at the employee lunch table. Help me remember that how I spend "my" discretionary moments can have a real, eternal impact on me or on someone else. Forgive me, Lord, for spending so much time ignoring the people around me. Hoarding my time on a Saturday afternoon or a Wednesday morning amounts to keeping my life rather than losing it for your sake—something that as a Christian I would likely vow up and down I don't do, at least not on a grand scale. Remind me that my grand scale is no more than the sum of its moments.

■ March 18

Father, I honestly think that in my quest for spiritual maturity I have departed on course from "point A." But often I am uncertain where "point B" is! Without that knowledge, I am bound to float unsatisfactorily in a kind of personal and spiritual limbo. When I am doing that, consciously or not, and am lacking clear goals, guide me. Reveal my point B, or at least the next few yards on the path toward it. Help me move toward the goal of maturity with dedication rather than shrugging my shoulders and using the excuse, "Perfection is impossible, so what I am doing is probably okay."

▰ March 19

As spring approaches, Lord God, I see early signs of its full-fledged beauty around me. I see perky little birds finding food in neighborhood yards and alongside parkways in the business sector. I see buds on some plants and blossoms on others. And I know that in addition to the outward beauty of these things is a hidden beauty in the amazing processes beneath the surface: nutrients feeding the grass that will spring up out of its dormancy and ants and other creatures living in their underground communities, aerating the soil. You have created a miraculous world! Thank you for extending your love to me through the re-creation I witness every spring.

▰ March 20

Savior God, strength to persevere and keep up the pace of life is almost more of a need during long stretches of "average" living than it is in times of high crisis. In the crises, friends have been asked to pray. Family may be on hand to help. Lord, we have a *dire* need to pray for strength on days when all seems fine. Appearance is deceiving. What seems ordinary often conceals brewing turmoil. I greatly desire to see you counteract the hidden, incubating turmoil that I cannot identify in my own heart and in the lives and plans of family members and others! Call me to pray for these things more often, trusting the particulars to you.

▰ March 21

Sustain me, loving Father, when I do not feel up to the steady beat of a productive, on-track life! I may hear the cadence, "Left! Right! Left! Right!" I may be going through the motions and doing the required things, but what if I find no great pleasure or deep and comforting spiritual insight on a given day? Am I letting you down? Or is it possible that my own joy or next brilliant idea is simply developing behind the scenes? When I feel blasé, pour your grace over me so I can keep up my basic duties. And "restore to me the joy of your salvation" (Ps. 51:12). I need this joy just as critically as I need food, water, and air!

▰ March 22

Help me, Lord, when I need courage not just for important work presentations and professional licensing exams, but for telling a family member, "I know I have not appreciated you as you deserve to be appreciated" and for answering with a firm "no" when my kids ask for something it would be easy for me to give them in spite of an inner tug at my conscience. If the wherewithal to do these things were easy to summon, it wouldn't be called *courage,* defined by *Webster's* as "mental or moral strength." It would be called something that meant "mental or moral *mediocrity,*" and who needs more of that?

▰ March 23

Lord Jesus, you didn't stop loving your disciples when they failed you by falling asleep although you'd asked them to watch and pray. You stood by them although they did not always stand by you. You patiently allowed for their weaknesses, then revealed your power, calling them out as potent missionaries. I am very thankful that you don't give up on me either when in self-centeredness and attentiveness to trivial, temporary things I just don't grasp and apply matters of faith in as many ways as possible. Reveal my true priorities! Show me what it means for you to be on the throne of my heart in each twenty-four-hour period on my calendar.

▬ March 24

Thank you, God, for repeated and obvious proof that your Word is true, cutting right to the heart of a matter. Help me to punctuate my conversation with more truth from Scripture. I don't have to sound like a preacher, stating chapter and verse. I just want to sound like, and *be*, a "salt and light" Christian wherever I happen to be. Proverbs 12:16 says it is a prudent person who lets an offense go by. Next time I encounter a road hog or a tailgater, I don't want my children to hear me state my *opinion* that it's safer and wiser not to retaliate—they need to hear from my lips that *God's Word* says so.

▬ March 25

I admit, Lord, that I can get very warm and happy looking back. Often I would rather re-experience something I know was good than venture out in search of a *new* good thing. It's comfort versus risk. I know you know I need comfort, but caution me not to linger in my cozy cocoon lined with favorite old books, favorite old TV shows, and favorite old memories so long that my eyes and my heart miss something in the path ahead—something, or someone, that will make my life richer and more dynamic if I march forward.

▬ March 26

Dear Lord, Hebrews 3:13 instructs us to encourage one another while it is still called "today." Remind us as we strive to reach our elusive "point B" that we have something important to do here and now, today. Let me never forget to live today as I reach toward tomorrow! Open my eyes to the opportunities I have to express encouragement, either seriously or humorously, by telephone, by letter, by e-mail, and especially in person. Remind me that encouragement is always needed, even when there is no outward sign of discouragement. Prompt me to encourage my family and friends with words, smiles, and hugs.

▄ March 27

I notice, dear God and Author of Scripture, that a number of psalms conclude with expressions of praise even after long, anguished tirades. Make me more like that, praising even when I feel downcast, confused, and forgotten. What is praiseworthy about you, God, does not change. And even though I feel unhappy at times, I want to be willing to praise you. I may not do it well. I may not praise with a smile, but I will praise. I understand that to praise you is a need within me; that need does not change because I am in a dark valley. I will not withdraw my belief that you are faithful to me.

▄ March 28

Lord, when I awaken at a quiet hour and realize a song has been going through my head as I move into full consciousness, I am amazed at the working of the mind! When that song is a Christian song, I need to pay attention, understanding that I have been given a gift to which my response can mean the making or breaking of my day! Forgive me for when I have viewed that morning song merely as mental overflow. Thank you for sending important words to me in the dark stillness, when nothing else was shouting for my attention. I need the quiet whispers of your Spirit.

▰ March 29

Sometimes, Father, when I drive past strangers who are in other vehicles or standing near the road, I want to shout through the windshield, "God loves you! He is in charge! Do you know that?" And I want to pray for them—but what should I say? Well, these strangers have the same needs I have. They struggle with choices, attitudes, and all the basic human stuff. So I will pray for them as I do for myself. Lord, I must not ignore what is on my left and on my right as I proceed to complete my busy agenda on a given day!

▰ March 30

Thank you, God, for my physical ability to sweep, dust, cook, and do laundry. I know there are many who would be glad to do these things if they could. I also realize that you do care about things as "insignificant" as my attitude toward housework. Lord, you care about my little issues, and so much more about the big challenges and messy ordeals. Lord, I am utterly dependent on you in all of these things. As I daily sift through the big, small, special, and ordinary stuff, remind me of the main thing: You are God, and I belong to you forever!

▰ March 31

Psalm 87:5 reads, "the Most High himself will establish [Zion]." When the Most High establishes something, it is firmly established, irrevocably begun to never end—unlike businesses that go bankrupt and marriages that are legally dissolved. Everlasting God, when *you* say "forever," you mean it! You have established your kingdom forever. You also have established forever *my place* in your kingdom. John 10:28 declares, "No one will snatch [my sheep] out of my hand." I walk in security because of that promise, Father, and I don't have enough words to thank you. Please hear the gratitude surging through my heart! Keep me walking in security—left, right, left, right—as I do my part and leave the role of commander to you.

55

april

seize the flowers

Yet you do not even know what tomorrow will bring. What is your life? For you are a mist that appears for a little while and then vanishes.

JAMES 4:14

april morning glory

One morning I prepared for work the way I'm prone to do,
My actions systematic and my route familiar, too.
But as I drove, that April morn, my eyes beheld a treat
In form of flowers bordering the winding, narrow street.
A charming sight against the green, and I began to think
They looked like giant buttercups—not gold, but
    palest pink.
Delightful little clusters well adorned that city strand
And greatly blessed an otherwise ungainly piece of land.
Unsightly buildings mattered not—not like those lovely plants
Which, neither sown nor kept by man, deserved my grateful
    glance.
A sudden impulse beckoned me, and swiftly I obeyed;
The moment would have come and quickly gone had I delayed.
A gravel drive ahead, a spot I'd never really seen,
Proved large enough to park my car and park my dull routine.
Before another soul appeared along that busy lane,
I'd seized a fist of flowers and was on my way again.
I took them to my destination, placed them on my desk,
And all that day they made the picture much more picturesque.
Next afternoon, I traveled home along that stretch of road
And saw with some regret that all the flowers had been mowed.
How glad I was I'd filled that whim the very day before,
And clutched the beauty in my path that now was there no more,

Instead of taking precious time to weigh the pro and con
And find with disappointment that the chance to act was gone.
Now, when I see I'm keeping lively impulse boxed away,
I try to put into the rut a greater sense of play;
To keep that box in easy reach, at times remove the lid,
The less to say *I wish I had*, the more to say *I did*.
I gently fight conformity and imitate the day
I stopped to pick the flowers that I saw along the way.

▰ April 1

Lord, how can my words possibly describe your greatness? They can't. They can't describe your goodness, either, but there are times when I am moved to try, with my words, to tell a friend or relative how good you have been to me, blessing me and ministering to me at my point of deepest need. Because you are great and good, I want to worship you today by living in a manner appropriate to one who calls herself your child. Speak gentle and encouraging words through my mouth. Let my face mirror grace and joy rather than looking stressed-out or dejected. Please pour upon me right now your presence, your power, and your peace for this day.

▰ April 2

Today is a precious gift, Lord God, and gifts should be received with appreciation and acknowledged promptly. Sad and plenteous are the stories of hurt feelings caused by the failure to say "thank you" for a gift chosen carefully or even made by hand for the recipient. Sometimes our hurt feelings are nursed into lifelong grudges. Forgive us, dear Lord, for the times we have failed to send a note or place a phone call to thank someone who paid us an undeserved kindness or gave us a thoughtful gift. Help us forgive the ones who have treated us this way, and help us train our children to consider thank-you expressions obligatory, not optional.

▰ April 3

Father God, guide me to "seize the flowers" so I don't miss available joys along this fast and fearsome path. Guide me also to seize the day for what can be gained and given. I dream of embarking on big projects and completing them, and if I don't do a little bit on those projects *today,* my dreams will stay unfulfilled. I like dreaming big, Lord! You've been calling ordinary people to extraordinary tasks for many centuries. Guide my dreams. I want your Holy Spirit to lead me in carrying out the valid ones and abandoning the pointless ones. Thank you for caring about my dreams and about me!

▄ April 4

Dear Lord, if I knew, suspected, or feared I had only a few days left to live on this earth, I would want to do a number of things with great urgency. If I set out to make a Top 10 list of those things, the list would fill up rather quickly. Guide me to make that list and discuss it with you. You might want me to reconsider some of the things on it. When I make the list, call me to pray over it, then guide me to take care of some of that "final" business now, while there is time to do so without panic and haste. Some of the people I should say important things to may not be here when I really am living my last days.

▄ April 5

When I ponder how brief life is, Savior God, I don't want to confuse myself regarding what to do about that. No extremes, first convincing myself I should do fifty million nice things for other people, then deciding I should do whatever makes *me* the most satisfied. Somewhere between the two extremes is a place for me. Not a fixed place, but a fluid one, incorporating generosity and thoughtfulness but also a healthy amount of attention to my own needs. And steer me away from thinking that the only issue associated with the brevity of life is what I do. *Who I am* is just as important, and *whose I am* is even more important!

■ April 6

Today, Lord, someone needs to hear from me, "You are valuable. You have wonderful qualities. You matter." Probably no one hears that enough at the most critical moments of self-doubt, yet it is also important to realize that we cannot be convinced of our own worth by the praises of others. Our worth comes from the one who created us. You, God, are the source of our value. When we understand that, we can accept ourselves as having intrinsic worth. Then we are able to behave with a confidence that can withstand personal failure. Build in us an attractive confidence based on faith! Let us draw others to you in that confidence rather than trying to paint a pretty facade over a structure built with faulty materials.

■ April 7

"Lord, keep your arm around my shoulder and your hand over my mouth!" So goes a well-put T-shirt message. Your Word proclaims our need for that message repeatedly. Proverbs 11:12 says, "Whoever belittles another lacks sense, but an intelligent person remains silent." Help me to remember that verse in the football stands next fall when "that kind of talk" starts. (Okay, I admit it. Sometimes I'm the one who starts it.) Father, everything I hear does not need to be repeated, even when I know it's true, and especially when it's secondhand gossip. By your Spirit, keep most of what goes in my ears from coming out my mouth.

■ April 8

Jesus, "when he was abused, . . . did not return abuse; when he suffered, he did not threaten; but he entrusted himself to the one who judges justly" (1 Peter 2:23). How short I fall of that example when I display my ability to volley trash talk back and forth with the best of them! Enable me to trust myself to your wisdom when it comes to being vindicated, God. Proverbs declares emphatically that the wicked will not go unpunished and will earn no real gain through their schemes, while those who sow righteousness get a true reward (Prov. 11:18–21). Your Word is trustworthy!

▰ April 9

How painful a heart of compassion can be, Father God! You know that. It was compassion that placed you on a criminal's cross in the person of Jesus. It was compassion that kept you from saying, "I wash my hands of you people." You made me in your image, Lord. Your heart is the source of my compassion. Yet my compassion has limits: limits of time, ability, and even willingness. I'm so thankful that your compassion is great enough to offer salvation through the sacrifice of Jesus. This is far beyond my understanding, Father. Only by faith can I accept it.

▰ April 10

I praise you, Father in heaven, for the fact that Jesus is alive! Alive not only in our memories and hearts the way we say certain beloved people remain alive after they have died, but alive in *fact*. Resurrected! Not having any idea what that intense burst of resurrection glory was really like, I imagine it must have been so bright and so physically significant—like a visual earthquake— that perhaps it was what awakened those who returned to Jesus' tomb early in the day and discovered that it held him no longer. Thank you that the unsealing of the tomb that first Easter morning *sealed* the verdict pronounced upon me, "Not guilty!"

■ April 11

Lord, I wish they would make a new reality TV show at my house called "Mildew Killers!" Remind me to contact a producer about it. Some of the dirtiest corners of my house could be used as a testing lab for the claims of various cleaning products on the market. They need exposure to "industrial strength" cleansers! Father, some of the most neglected corners of my life need exposure to *resurrection strength cleansing power.* Today produce in me a closer likeness of you. Give me personal victory today over the hidden traps waiting to get me.

■ April 12

Lord, one reason we are able to live one day at a time is that you, in your wisdom and mercy, have concealed what tomorrow holds. Thank you for sparing us the anguish of knowing in advance when tragedy will occur; thank you also for concealing when good things will happen so that today's emotions are not overloaded with tomorrow's joys and pleasant surprise is not eliminated from our experience. If we were to know future events, we would not be functional in the present. Thank you, Lord, for the gift of today and the gift of the inability to see over the horizon into tomorrow. We walk by faith, not by sight. Give me more faith so I will worry less about tomorrow and be able to enjoy today!

■ April 13

Lord of all things, Lord of my heart, teach me to forgive others as you forgive me. Make my life a greater factor in reducing hostility and establishing positive relationships. In the "little" matters of the home, Lord, let me take a stand for true forgiveness—a stand my husband and children will notice, benefit from, and eventually imitate. As much as I strive to eliminate conflict, I can't always do that. When conflict occurs, lead me away from anger and grudges. Forgiveness is difficult to live out, Lord. I need your almighty power to improve on that—today.

■ April 14

Encouragement, Lord, is something I need to seize more unashamedly from sources available to me. It is something I want to give away more often to the people in my world. Give me an encouraging word and a smile to share with someone who needs it today. Lead me to write personal notes, too. How special it is to receive a note in the mail with thoughtful, personalized words! Because I know how valuable that is to the receiver, let me be more diligent in being the giver. Written and mailed correspondence is an endangered species. I thank you that it's not extinct. Bless those who do ministry through their personal correspondence.

■ April 15

Halfway through the month, it occurs to me, patient and loving Father, *Do I often stop at the halfway point when I pray?* I fear that I do. I may plead intently a few times, then forget the passion with which I poured a situation out before you. I ask in anguish, "Why, why?" and do not pay attention to how receptive I am being to an answer. My attention span is short. My actions in prayer betray a trust level that needs to grow. Call me to more persistent praying, Lord, and teach me to understand your ways and your answers. Assure me of your love, your presence, your comfort, and your control over all things.

▰ April 16

God, I am sometimes puzzled by the lack of change in situations or people I pray for. Is there a problem with my faith? Am I not persistent in praying? Do I not understand your will? Is there a hidden sin in the way in my life as the pray-er or in theirs as the pray-ee? Am I just being impatient, the victim of a culture-born demand for instant satisfaction? It's said that prayer doesn't change things, it changes people. I see the truth of that statement as I look back over my life. If I am the thing that needs changing now, show me how I must change. Show me how to lose myself more and more in you and trust all things to you.

▰ April 17

Today, Father God, I ask you for guidance in ending procrastination on one issue. It may be at work or at church or at home. It may be a matter of personal organization and task-juggling priority. Whether it is relational and huge, like a parent/child forgiveness issue, or as practical and small as cleaning out the junk closet, I would like the satisfaction of saying, *"It is accomplished."* And in my quest to conquer procrastination, direct my timing. I can't take care of *every* task and every broken relationship today. The opportunity must be right, my approach must be reasonable and sensitive, and your Spirit must be in control.

▰ April 18

Lord, build in me the skill of waiting patiently for the calculated blessings you are preparing for me on your timetable. In this culture we have become impatient over one-minute computer operations, two-minute traffic lights, and three-minute microwave dinners. We find it difficult to wait days for a special event, think it's backward to wait six weeks for a natural tan, and consider it almost unheard-of to wait years for a strong love relationship to develop. It was not always so! Lord, let the inspiring stories of patience and perseverance be not just in the Bible and in novels but in today's newspapers and in my personal journal.

■April 19

Lord, show me how to think "big picture" when frustrations and worries are close to home. I don't want to look back someday and see I have spent my brief time with tunnel vision, clawing desperately for something elusive while ignoring good things and other opportunities all around me. Help me trust long-term outcomes to you! Trusting can be a real hurdle, Lord, but I believe you are worthy of my trust. Help me to trust you more so I can honestly know peace in a mixed-up world. You are great enough to attend to your creation, even to the tiniest details, including the details of my life today and tomorrow.

■April 20

Technology allows us to do much more in much less time, yet we seem always rushed and seldom content! Father, resurrect in us the ability to see more of what we are racing past in our haste to get someplace else. Have we lost the "back porch in summertime" scenario forever? Perish the thought. Give us a greater capacity for spending longer periods of time with people without requiring artificial noise and pre-fab entertainment to fill the space and the time. I long for the romanticized aspects of a slower-paced era. Grant us, Lord, more contentment in the present era. Grant us peace in our souls and peace with you.

▰ April 21

Today is here, Lord. There is only one of it, and in twenty-four hours it will be history. Father, the history that this day is destined to become will not be recorded, in finality, for hours yet. Though already work has been done, decisions have been made, thoughts have been completed, and failings have been committed, time still remains to make certain that this day will go down in my spiritual history as a day of good, value, and victory. God, use the hours that remain of this day to draw me closer to you; to work in me, so I can become humbler, more thankful, and more joyful; and to work through me, so I can become more helpful and encouraging to others.

▰ April 22

Lord, delete forever from my vocabulary, and my thinking, these words: "If all else fails, pray," and "Well, all we can really do is pray." These expressions belittle the role and the significance of prayer. Forgive me for the times I've tried every solution in my power before it occurs to me to pray and ask for *your* power! Let me never think that praying about a situation is somehow not enough—that I should always pray *plus* do something else. "Putting feet to your prayers" is a valid concept at times, but sometimes the feet I think of putting to a prayer may be misguided. They may be a hindrance. Help me know when I should simply pray and leave the practical details to your wisdom and authority.

▰ April 23

"This is the day that the LORD has made; let us rejoice and be glad in it" (Ps. 118:24). Lord, help me rejoice not only in the day, but also in the fact that you have made the day. But what if I don't feel glad about a given day, Lord, nor glad even about the fact that you have made the day? Is guilt for being spiritually immature to be added to my misery? Help me at those times. And when I talk to people who respond to this verse with scorn, make me especially sensitive. If nothing I say comforts them, then would you please comfort them as only you can?

■ April 24

God, give me the good sense to use nonwork days not only to accomplish those "weekend projects" but also to seize the day to laugh and be childlike. I mean, why should playing with sidewalk chalk and stuffed animals be just for kids? And even if my "letting go" activities are never quite that juvenile, let me go about them with a more youthful attitude. Children suspect that freedom and fun begin when they get older, yet growing up seems to bring more responsibility than freedom and more obligation than fun. Have I gradually exchanged fun for worry? Have I forgotten how to be lighthearted over the fact that you are my Champion? God, forbid it to be so.

■ April 25

Father, you created in us a need for rest. Let me never be afraid to say, "Today I accomplished something very important. I rested. *All day long!*" Lord, even when the value of rest is recognized, achieving more of it rarely seems an option; what can be cut out to make room for a nap, a longer night's sleep, or a quiet hour of tea and television? Some proudly proclaim that sleep is a waste of time, a nuisance to be indulged in for as few hours as possible. When that attitude results in forced rest due to illness or burnout, we wake up to the truth about sleep! In your great patient love, restore our health and our common sense when that happens.

▰ April 26

Dear Lord, some things that bother us about life, death, good, and evil will not be changed until the time you have appointed, but I believe you want us to have more victory *now* and be more empowered *now* to improve particular situations. Show me the way to victory, Lord, for my own needs and those of the people I care about. I want to seize the day in spiritual matters as well as in physical work and play. Show me how to draw more of your power out of the "if only" realm into the "see what God has done" realm! Call me to knowledgeable, confident prayer for these things!

▰ April 27

God, you are with me "like a dread warrior" (Jer. 20:11). Whatever the assignment, let me be useful in your war effort. Keep me from cluelessness and stubborn disobedience in small things so I may be fit for you to give me even bigger tasks. And always keep me aware that "big" does not necessarily mean visible to masses of people. Remind me, Lord, that the battle is not mine, but yours. Strengthen me to act according to your battle plan. Show me the people I need to pray for, and move my heart and mouth accordingly. Remind me that I am not an uncertain and lone warrior but a member of a mighty army whose victory is promised!

▰ April 28

Sometimes, Lord, other people's words are right on target for what I need to express. Let me not feel shy about repeating someone else's words in praise of you. After all, that's been done for centuries in public and private worship as Scripture is read and hymns are sung, with the words falling like sweet drops of life on eager ears and seeking hearts. Please keep my ears and my heart eager and seeking, Lord. Don't let me be fooled into thinking I've heard it all. (Even if I've heard it, I've forgotten most of it!) I need to hear words of faith and Scripture again and again, just as I need to hear "I love you" regularly from someone I already know loves me.

▰ April 29

Dear Father, I thank you that one of the joys of today is the fun of planning and dreaming for tomorrow. I believe planning ahead is a desire and ability that comes from you, Lord, even though I have no guarantee that particular plans will be fulfilled exactly as hoped or expected. Give me balance between trusting the future to you and participating in the planning of my future. I must not live exclusively in the past, the present, or the future. I need to understand all three and consider them wisely. Let me evaluate and learn from the past. Let me seize and cherish the present. Let me dream of future possibilities and anticipate them with joy!

▰ April 30

Father, I see trouble and strife everywhere. I am tempted to say, "The needs will never go away, and nothing I do will make a real difference." I know I can make a difference if you want me to. Let my prayers, words, and actions make a difference for the benefit of other people. Pull me back and give me a better grip on the realities I'm dealing with. Make me leave to you what I shouldn't be trying to deal with at all. Remind me that life is not a sprint but a marathon. If I am always rushing and if I have a narrow definition of "accomplishment," I will miss blessings and fail to see needs I can meet. Strengthen me, Lord, and guide me in the next segment of the journey.

may

bringing heavenly realities down to earth

Do you not realize that God's kindness is meant to lead you to repentance?

ROMANS 2:4

■ May 1

Almighty God, we are blessed by your kindness long before we are aware of it and in many ways that we never realize. Let us seek and accept your kindness with the understanding that it is meant to lead us to repentance (Rom. 2:4). Repentance is not the popular answer to sin. We would rather justify our sin and spend a lot of time pointing out the bad influences in our lives that have predisposed us to do what we are doing. At worst we refuse to show remorse but instead flaunt for applause the kind of living that polite society once found repugnant. Convict us of our sin. Recreate in us the capacity for shame.

■ May 2

Thank you, God, for sending Jesus to provide forgiveness because we had a place in your heart before you had a place in ours. Thank you for being greater than anything that happens and for promising never to abandon us! These are the spiritual realities we need in our lives. When a parent is dying of cancer, a child is killed in an accident, a neighbor is called away to war—or when there is no big crisis but it is still difficult to find the energy to get out of bed—we need your comfort and your presence. Reveal that our discontent is a spiritual condition, not merely a human given. Reveal yourself as the source of true peace and everlasting love.

■ May 3

Scripture and human lives give us overwhelming testimony that you are a good and loving God, yet many doubt or deny it. We need assurance that you are good, loving, in control, and waiting eagerly to receive all who call out to you sincerely. Please send this assurance when we struggle with hardship and fail to understand why you allow it. Remind us, Lord, that bad circumstances do not have to threaten what we believe about your goodness. Keep us firmly convinced of your love and goodness, regardless of the present details of our lives and the questions we cannot answer.

▰ May 4

Lord, you are good and loving. You are also holy, all-powerful, and a dispenser of judgment. No wonder the prophet Isaiah cried out, "Woe is me!" when he saw that incredible vision of you in the temple (Isa. 6:5)! You are *Almighty God, the infinite Creator.* I am the finite and helpless created one, yet you have drawn me into significance before you. You have valued human beings above other forms of creation and have invited us to come to you by salvation through the blood of Jesus. This is impossible to grasp except by faith. Increase my faith, I pray, so I will live with more heavenly reality in my down-to-earth life.

▰ May 5

Father, thank you for this majestic statement about the reality of who Jesus is: "He is the image of the invisible God . . . He himself is before all things, and in him all things hold together . . . he is the beginning, the firstborn from the dead, so that he might come to have first place in everything" (Col. 1:15, 17–18). Reality check! Does Jesus have first place on my to-do list? In my credit history? My radio presets? My marriage? (Am I as fervent in my praying for my husband as for myself?) Father, if Jesus has first place, his words and his example will permeate what I think and do. Convince me once and for all that if I don't read the Bible more than a few minutes in church each week, I will never know enough about Jesus to really *get it*.

▰ May 6

Jesus, you are Lord! You are also God, the only one with the power to erase sin's marks and declare a person clean. That's an exclusive claim, Lord, in a day when eclectic spirituality is very popular and rejection of another's religion is considered narrow-minded. I don't want to be embarrassed to stand up for the exclusive claim of Christ, and I need not be, because with exclusive claim comes inclusive invitation: "For God . . . gave his only Son, so that *everyone* who believes in him may not perish but may have eternal life" (John 3:16). "Then everyone who calls on the name of the Lord will be saved" (Acts 2:21).

▰ May 7

"Happy are those whose transgression is forgiven, whose sin is covered" (Ps. 32:1). Happy? Am I happy that I have been forgiven? Absolutely. Do I think about that very often? Hmm. Perhaps one of my worst sins, holy and gracious Father, is failing to thank you every day for forgiving my sins. *Happy*. What a word. It describes a feeling that comes and goes many times every day. "Here's the bracelet you wanted. Happy?" "Yes, thank you!" God, give me the same excited delight and eagerness to "show and tell" regarding my forgiven state that I have regarding new clothes and new career moves.

▰ May 8

Thank you, heavenly Father, for my mother and for other women who have mothered me. Thank you for the dedication of mothers to nurturing and protecting their children. Thank you for their compassionate hearts and listening ears. A season of special remembrance brings precious sentiments from a mother's family. But from you a mother needs energy, rest, peace of mind, and faith every day of the year! To the mother who gives so much of herself, grant sufficient time for her own well-being. Watch over expectant mothers. Comfort grieving mothers and those whose desire to be a mother has not been realized. Help us love our mothers and remember with thankfulness the mothers who are no longer with us. Thank you for Mary, the mother of our Lord Jesus, who heard and obeyed your special call.

May 9

Lord, I know you care about the details of my job, my relationships, and my habits. I have evidence upon evidence that you are paying attention to all these things. But please don't stop there! Work on *me,* not just on my situations. Heavenly power needs to get into my earthly reality when I am "chatting" (gossiping) at the ball field, "conversing" (arguing) with my husband, "remembering" (hating) someone who once hurt me, and "thinking" (stressing) about what I have to do next week. Pour your power over me, God. I ask you this in faith, believing that you will change me, making me stronger for you.

May 10

Thank you, precious God, for the gift of salvation by grace through faith. I know I am saved by grace alone, not by any intrinsic or acquired personal worth and not by my actions. I want to do good works for you, not to achieve salvation but out of devotion to you. Help me, Lord, not to grow weary and lose the joy of serving because I'm continually wondering if my work for you is "enough." It is not about amounts and tally marks but about availability and spiritual growth. Call me to do what I can do, and bless the service I offer to you.

■ May 11

Help me, heavenly Father, not to be motivated excessively by concern over others' opinions of me and by fear of disappointing someone with my decisions. On the other hand, I don't believe it's always correct to say, "It doesn't matter what others think," because Scripture points out the need to consider how our actions affect others. Lord, give me wisdom in these things. I love you and I want to please you. Reveal your will to me and help me obey it. In the process, let "what others may think of me" come to mean exactly what it should mean to me—no more and no less.

■ May 12

Father God, culture has worked in us a notion that *following* shows weakness. We don't want to be led. We want to be independent, free to pursue our own lives. We don't want to be led astray by an unworthy leader with good intentions or tricked by a liar. So, Lord, give us parents, teachers, church leaders, supervisors, CEOs, elected officials, and friends who will lead us according to your will. And when we recoil from following *you,* Lord, show us the error of trying to be gods to and among ourselves.

■ May 13

Precious Lord, I cherish the freedom to assemble for worship. Give me more freedom from what goes on inside of me to hinder my worship. I often approach worship as I do the workday or a football game: *How's my hair? Is this outfit okay? Who's here? Who's not here? What's on the schedule after this?* Lord, when next I enter a public worship place, call me to recognize it as holy. Call me in that place to honor you with a humble heart and a seeking mind. Make plain your message through Word and song. Give me a truth I can latch onto—something that will improve my attitude toward myself, my family, and my hectic routine.

▉ May 14

Heavenly Father, prepare me to do what 1 Peter 3:15 instructs: "Always be ready to make your defense to anyone who demands from you an accounting for the hope that is in you." Make me aware that another's demand for an accounting of my hope may not be a direct question. It may be buried in a hostile e-mail message; it may appear in an off-the-cuff remark I hear in a crowd. When I recognize a need for assurance or for basic information that I may be able to provide, help me respond with prayer and perhaps with appropriate words offered in kindness, not superiority.

▉ May 15

Lord, help me handle minor and major problems with a growing faith and good coping skills. Especially for the benefit of impressionable children, make my off-the-cuff reaction to traffic problems and spilled beverages less nasty and more easygoing. When I have water-damaged floors, I will let you know I am upset, but I vow to you I will also be thankful for all that *isn't* wrong. I don't want to buy into a mindset that everything bad is completely and irredeemably bad. I don't want to be remembered by my children as a sour and impatient person. Help me glean from my bad experiences the learning that can be gleaned. Help me use trouble to understand someone else's trouble later on.

▪ May 16

Blessed and holy God, you have called us to be "special utensils, dedicated and useful . . . , ready for every good work" (2 Tim. 2:21). When I scramble eggs, the cleanup is aggravating. Dried egg isn't removed by the usual scrubbing; it has to be scraped off. Like a kitchen spatula, my heart and mind need cleaning. I tend not to think of that very often. I tend to forget that even a blood-cleansed believer gets dirty along the path to heaven. Who has time to recognize and confess sin when life is so busy with work and play? Lord, call me to greater seriousness about this. Keep me ready and useful.

▪ May 17

Holy God, while it is wonderful to focus on your gift of salvation, I mustn't forget about my responsibility. Second Chronicles 29:5 speaks of sanctifying oneself and the house of the Lord, removing filth from the holy place. Filth? Really, now. It's just a bad habit. It's a weakness I'm sure is inherited. It's just sarcasm (meant in fun!). It's harmless; just shopaholism. It's just snobbery. It's . . . *filth*. Teach me intolerance of my sin, Lord! My behavior is so much more than where work and errands take me. It is how my mind works, how I love my family, and how much value I assign in my heart of hearts to the people crowded into the super-everything store on Saturday.

▬ May 18

"But seek after selfishness, annoyance, gossip, derision, shallowness, apathy, and fear. These are good things." A far cry from what Scripture really teaches! But, Lord, a steady routine of "reality" TV shows, pleasure reading, pop rock music, Internet surfing, and weekly movie rentals does not develop Spirit-given traits in us. None of these hobbies is necessarily sinful. The sin is in letting the frenzied pursuit of personal "R and R" consume every minute of our discretionary time, leaving us in a state of secularized Christianity and perpetual spiritual infancy because we never pray or read our Bibles. Blessed are those whom you enable to realize that and to escape the trap. Find me in that group!

▬ May 19

Thank you, God, for the promise and the reality of abundant life through Jesus! Thank you that abundant life includes joy and peace, Christian friendship, excitement over how you are working all over the world, spirit-lifting public and private worship, release from destructive thinking and behaving, and the ability to love with a love that comes from your heart. Abundant life is the relief of knowing my sins are forgiven. Abundant life is finding pure pleasures to enjoy even though life is not purely pleasurable at all times. Abundant life is grace to survive and cope when life is not pleasurable. Thank you, Lord Jesus, for coming that we may have life and have it abundantly (John 10:10)!

▬ May 20

Lord Jesus, as a human being I have difficulty giving you control of my body and my mind. Take control! You are completely holy; you became fully human and struggled between the two natures, yet were without sin. Thank you for willingly entering that state of conflict, submissive to the culture and eventually to ruthless political and judicial powers. Jesus, you understand what it is like to be frustrated, angry, hurt, annoyed, grief-stricken, stressed, creative, joyful, and all the rest. Minister to me, precious Jesus, as I strive to be holy while also having no choice but to be human.

▰ May 21

Father, help me accept what the Bible teaches about life and eternity even if I cannot understand all aspects of it. Remind me daily that most of what I can see with my eyes is temporary. So much of it is wonderful to see, Lord! Remind me that creation, though beautiful, is here only for a purpose and a time you have established. When the time comes to let go of this present earth and my place in it, may it be revealed that my real grip was on the eternal things all along.

▰ May 22

Dear Lord, I have seen the evidence and the results of Satan's work in and around me. But you have issued armor and weapons for spiritual battle: truth, righteousness, the gospel of peace, faith, salvation, the Holy Spirit, your written Word, and prayer. Powerful weapons! Yet I forget to be armed and ready to do battle, in a loving spirit, when I am confronted with a teenager's rage, with false religious ideas, with secular values, and with the confusion of my own thoughts. Make the enemy's strategy plain to me so I will know when "my thoughts" are actually his whispered suggestions: *"That guy is a bum, totally worthless!" "I am so stupid!" "My child will never learn."* Receiving Satan's lies as my thoughts makes me a victim. Using spiritual weapons against those lies makes me a conqueror!

▬ May 23

All-powerful God, I want to be nowhere but on your team. I need a leader who does what you do! You speak the truth. You rescue and defend. You guide and comfort. You save souls and build people into their best selves. You love. The opponent is Satan, the personification of evil. He is a foe who deceives and oppresses. He creates feelings of worthlessness, envy, and spite. He causes sin, fear, worry, hate, and crime. He destroys everything he can. Scripture teaches this, Lord, and I see that it is true. But, God, the ultimate victory is yours! Open our eyes and let us be confident in the truth rather than feeling defeated.

▬ May 24

In other times and cultures, Lord, the spoken word carried much more weight. Vows were unbreakable. Blessings spoken by a patriarch were irrevocable. Verbal contracts were binding. Words are no less powerful today. Everyone knows the blessing of kind words and the damage of harsh words. "Death and life are in the power of the tongue," reads Proverbs 18:21. Let me not open the door for Satan's work by thoughtlessly predicting undesirable outcomes ("It's going to be a nasty confrontation") or carelessly making a joke ("I think I'm going to be sick that day"). Lord, make me very aware of the way I speak so I am not giving Satan permission to wreak havoc.

▬ May 25

Teach us, Lord, the reality of spiritual warfare. It isn't only about curses, demonic possession, compulsive antisocial behavior, and such. It goes on in every "little" area of life. An argument breaks out in the car. If we do not recognize Satan's work in our hearts and mouths, we go on accepting petty family squabbles as a fact of life that we "just can't help." We yell, fume silently, get over it, and go on, pretending it hasn't torn a brick from the foundation of our relationship. But it has. Spiritual warfare is all around us. Move us, O God, to wake up and get our armor on! By your Spirit, control our thoughts and our oh-so-powerful words.

▰ May 26

Dear Lord, a serious "us against them" mindset causes so much of our conflict! Young against old. Race against race. Female against male. Superior against subordinate. Much conflict stems from distrust, jealousy, and a struggle for "top dog" status. Where does this mindset come from? Satan, the deceiver. He is the source of conflict; it *isn't* the angry boss, the insensitive spouse, the ungrateful child, or the rude motorist! When I still find myself behaving as if "strange" people are to be avoided, authority figures are to be resented, and peers are competitors to be outsmarted, make me more inclusive, more deferent, and more kind.

▰ May 27

Lord God, when I am defeated and frustrated, remind me that the ruler of this world, Satan, will be driven out (John 12:31). Show me how he can be defeated even now, one battle at a time. When Satan turns my eye to the so-called greener grass that makes me scorn the blessings in my life, make me more grateful for what I have. I am not acting in a way that's pleasing to you, nor healthy for me or my family, if I invest energy in being convinced I am missing something "better." Help me stay committed to the vows I have made and the responsibilities I have sought. Give me a heart of gratitude for every good gift you have given me.

▬ May 28

Thank you, God, for our nation. You have been gracious to our country far beyond the extent to which we have honored you. Yet it was faith that led to the stamping of "In God We Trust" on our coins. It was allegiance to you that placed "one nation, under God" in our pledge of allegiance to the flag. Call us back to our spiritual roots, Lord, as a nation founded on faith "whose God is the LORD" (Ps. 33:12) and which is moved to repentance because of your incredible kindness. Guide our military. Give courage and comfort to men and women who work for national security and defense.

▬ May 29

What an awful outfit! I wish I had her figure. Too much makeup. Bad hair! Lord, such thoughts run through my brain at the market, at work, and, of course, at the mall. Even at church! Give me the maturity to take a sincere interest in who people are, not how they present themselves. Appraising appearances is part of a "compare and compete" attitude that feeds my ego while proving I am shallow and insecure. It also makes me justify my present state instead of trying to improve myself. If I decide that my 20-pound excess is not all that bad because that person over there could drop 45 pounds, I am missing the real issue: my stewardship of my body, which is your temple. If I must compare, remind me to compare myself to Jesus.

▬ May 30

Father, I want to forgive others, but I have deep wounds and a good memory. I also have trouble forgiving *myself.* Humanly speaking, it helps when the years distance us from a regrettable

85

past. But the amount of time since a forgiven sin was committed does not matter to you. It is *distance* that matters: you remove our sin from us as far as the east is from the west (Ps. 103:12). What a beautiful image! Remind us of it when Satan torments us with guilt and embarrassment over our mistakes. He wants us to believe we *can't* be forgiven so we won't even bother to come to you and ask. Through Jesus, free us from our sins, and free us to forgive others.

▰ May 31

Psalm 16:11 proclaims, "In your presence there is fullness of joy; in your right hand are pleasures forevermore." Thank you, gracious God, for the fact that forgiveness puts heaven in my grasp! How wonderful it will be to have no more sickness, sadness, death, greed, disparagement, or conflict; no boredom, no competition to be heard, no forgetfulness, no worry; nothing to be upset by; and no shortage of time. Most of all, you will be there! God, give me greater anticipation of heaven, and give me more of your presence right now as I seek you with all of my heart.

june

dreams have a place in reality!

What is impossible for mortals is possible for God.

LUKE 18:27

▰ June 1

Lord God, I long for many things. I long to see things that I have honestly considered "unlikely" become reality. Sometimes I have prayed to observe or experience your presence and your power "in an unusual way." Actually, I would like to see what I now think of as unusual become more usual. Motivate my behavior so that prayer becomes more a constant pattern for me than a sometime device I use "when I need it." I need it constantly! Mature my praying as I study your Word. Help me realize my dream of being pleasing and useful to you.

▰ June 2

Increase my faith, O Lord, so I will have more hope and more confidence as I pray and as I live. God, to hope in you is vastly different from *hoping* a ball game won't be rained out. It is to have confident expectation of the things you have promised. Even more than that, it is to experience abundant life now rather than thinking that everything "better" begins later. When stressful circumstances drag on, assure me of your love and send your grace to be my sufficiency in a life that constantly shouts, "Insufficient!" in my face. My hope is in you and in you alone. Be the God of all my dreams and all of me.

▰ June 3

Lord, TV talk shows and library shelves are filled with material recommending ways to achieve the perfect love relationship, the ideal job, harmonious family ties, and business strategies that yield high performance and low conflict. Knowledge and effort are key ingredients in turning our best dreams into realities. First of all, change requires awareness that change is an option.

And change in our "impossible" situations requires the essential ingredient of the power of almighty God! All things are possible for you! Many things are possible for us, but many of them are not helpful for us, even though they might seem to be. Teach us, God, to entrust all of our dreams and needs to you.

▄June 4

Luke records at least two miraculous healings by Jesus to which the crowd's response was to glorify God. Teach me to glorify you, God, when I experience miracles. Forgive me for being blind or indifferent to the scores of miracles around me every day. As I plead for signs that you are working in the problem situations and troubled lives on my prayer list, teach me to trust details and outcomes to your infinite wisdom. My very existence is a miracle and a part of your good creation. I am in awe of your miraculous works! Increase my wonder at the things you have done. Increase my expectation of more great things from you.

▄June 5

Lord Jesus, the healings and other miracles you did were not a means of showing off. I believe their purpose was to demonstrate that you are God, and to demonstrate that a God whose power can restore a lame arm before people's eyes can also heal from sin the unseen soul inside each person. I believe, too, that you healed a blind man more because he called out to you in his need than because it was an appropriate time to teach a lesson to a crowd. We continue to ask for signs and wonders. Hear our cries for healing and for direction. Open our understanding when we become confused about the presence and purpose of your miracles in our lives.

▬ June 6

Lord Jesus, I do not have to dream of salvation as a hoped-for-but-not-necessarily-guaranteed event. Clearly you have promised that the repentant plea for salvation is answered "Yes!" by a Father anxious to see sinners reconciled to himself. You are my Savior to the same degree today as on the day I first prayed for salvation. But I pray today that you will become my Lord to a greater degree than before. I have a few short years on this earth. Make those years count for you! Through all the working, driving, waiting, cooking, cleaning, mothering, daughtering, wife-ing, planning, crying, laughing, resting, and dreaming, teach me what it means to own you as Lord.

▬ June 7

When friends are gathered together for a fun time, it is a privilege to suggest, "Why don't we pray together before people start leaving?" God, give me courage and a sense of rightness, not pretentiousness, about doing that. It's reasonably common-place to say, "We sure need God's help in these troubled times," but it needs to go a step further, from need to action and from wanting more to asking more to having more. Your Word says we do not have because we do not ask (James 4:2). I am going to ask more and have more—not more things, but more of your power for victorious living.

▬ June 8

Lord, keep me childlike enough to dream big dreams, yet continue showing me what dreams are appropriate to a disciple of Christ. The place of dreams in the reality of a believer is not as one-faceted as having incredible visions come to pass occasionally or even frequently. My dreams must be scrutinized. Are they self-serving? Even if not, are they within your plan for my life? No matter what I desire, am I willing to forsake it entirely for you? I want to love you, God, and lose myself in you to the point that I am *willing* to give up what I want most, whether you ask me to do that or not. It's all about whose agenda I hold most sacred—yours or mine.

June 9

Wake me up, dear Lord, to the realities of transformed living in Christ, especially when true devotion to you is lost in a whirlwind lifestyle driven fast by secular materialism with a bit of faith thrown in as seasoning. Forgive me for asking all sorts of blessings from you while conveniently overlooking my need for daily confession of sin. If I'm convinced I don't have all that much to confess, perhaps I'm quite blind to my own imperfections. Reveal each of my suppressed and hidden sins to me, Lord God, so I can receive forgiveness and be an instrument for you instead of always thinking of myself as the one whose wishes should be your first priority.

June 10

Father in heaven, when drastic changes of fortune come along, the substance of our character is tested. Our faith may be revealed as either a circumstance we have accepted for years without much personal investment or a notion we have popularly associated with tangible blessing. When wonderful things happen beyond our expectation and when huge empires come crumbling down, make us realize what is the work of our hands and what is the work of you in us. In both honor and humiliation, we are completely in your hands. In success, keep us humble within and courteous without. In failure, keep us the same. In in-between, mundane living, keep us the same! Call us to be faithful servants no matter the circumstances.

▪ June 11

Lord God, our reality sometimes finds us asking, "Why should I love God? He has not demonstrated his love for me; he has not corrected the problems I've prayed so hard about!" Teach us to be sure of your love without trying to tie your love to "amounts" of blessing and burden. Help us when it feels as if you have not heard our cries. When we want to turn away from you in hurt and anger, at least let us turn to a caring person of faith whose love and prayers will eventually turn us back to you. You have promised never to leave us or forsake us (Heb. 13:5). Satan tells us the opposite; teach us not to listen to him!

▪ June 12

Father, I dream of peace. Peace is a constant theme of life. People crave it. They want the external fighting and the internal churning to stop. Paul wrote, "For he is our peace . . . and has broken down the dividing wall, that is, the hostility between us" (Eph. 2:14). I long for war and violence to cease. I dream of homes, workplaces, and schools where cruel speech is replaced by words that come from changed hearts. The power to change hearts comes from you alone, O God! Give me actions and words that prove you are changing me. Guide me to reduce hostility and facilitate peace.

▰ June 13

Dear Lord, you know what I'm thinking of when I refer to "asking for the moon." I want you to know every desire of my heart. In fact, you already know each one. And you know better than I do which desires should become realities. Help me trust you in that. Today I thank you for the personal dreams I've seen come true. I thank you for dreamlike realities in my life that I don't remember ever asking for but that you have given anyway. Today I'm not asking for anything more. I still have unfulfilled dreams, Lord. But I am deciding, for today, to be perfectly content. Your grace is sufficient for me.

▰ June 14

Lord God, I greatly desire to live in a nation whose mottoes ring true when they proclaim, "in God we trust" and "one nation, under God." On Flag Day and other patriotic days, renew our appreciation for political freedom. Renew our desire for spiritual freedom from wicked actions and thoughts. A government cannot mandate the kind of living you desire from us. Let us choose to love your commandments. If you have our hearts, right actions will follow. I passionately hope to see America come home to you, God!

▰ June 15

Help me and other women, O Lord, to love our husbands. Call us to support them in our prayers and in our practical service to them. Give us more love for them in spite of their faults and our own. Help us understand that when we deliberately choose the route of appropriate deference to our husbands, we encourage our children's ability to accept their fathers' authority. Give us godly men in our lives, men whose faith and life habits we can respect. Lord Jesus, I dream of more sons who can call their father their best friend. I dream of more daughters who want to marry men like their fathers.

June 16

Creator God, you have put into our human makeup the desire to set personal goals and work toward achieving them. We imagine ourselves becoming champion athletes, famous artists, successful inventors, or highly paid consultants. It is fun and motivational to set our sights high and see our hard work pay off with achievement and personal development. Help us encourage our children's dreams; keep us from pressuring them to achieve what we failed to achieve ourselves. Show us when we need to pull back and reevaluate our own dreams. Remind us that "big" dreams include many more issues than the kind of successes the world can see and applaud.

June 17

When I consider all that you suffered when you submitted to cruel beating, humiliation, and crucifixion, precious Jesus, I understand (in my very limited way) that you gave up a perfect paradise to endure the unimaginable agony that I deserved. You gave up everything for me. I owe my life to you. Make me more grateful for your grace and less expectant of blessings as if they were due to me. Lord Jesus, be Lord of my behavior as I strive to keep your commandments. Be Lord of my thoughts when I am tempted to be judgmental and scornful. Be Lord of my heart as I desire to love you because you sacrificed your life out of love for me.

▪ June 18

How nice it would be, Lord, if family life were a little more like one of those classic television shows. The children respect authority, use good manners, and usually learn a valuable lesson about right and wrong. Television is a far cry from reality on any given subject, but I am thankful for the content that can be a positive influence and an inspiration. As long as television is an important cultural influence, I ask you to allow Christian values a voice there. Help us find programming that depicts people encouraging one another, keeping promises, behaving with integrity and morality, and saying important things with courage and concern.

▪ June 19

Father God, you know all. You have a much broader and more wonderful plan than I am able to see or even imagine. Teach me that waiting on you does not have to be boringly passive or filled with impatient frustration. Help me trust you enough not to resent it when you ask me to wait. Show me the other business at hand while I am waiting. Prepare me. Teach me patience while also teaching me persistence. Your Word promises that those who wait on you will be blessed because they waited. Teach me to go the route that results in the most blessing! Teach me to turn all of my wants over to your holy will.

▪ June 20

The Bible declares, "I can do all things through him who strengthens me" (Phil. 4:13). I want to be able to do all things if you ask me to, Lord! I want to do all that's required and a whole lot that's optional! Much of what I do in this present life will not last. Still, it is required and important, and some of it will outlive me through what it has built in my children and in others. When my days are consumed with work, cooking, cleanup, child care, church activities, and hobbies, remind me that what I am doing is important. I'm not Superwoman, but I do Herculean amounts of activity in a given day's time. Strengthen me, Lord, I pray!

▇ June 21

Thank you, God, for Christian ministries that address homelessness, abuse, poverty, crisis pregnancy, terminal illness, divorce, and other struggles. Many of these ministries are dreams in action for persons in whom you have sparked the desire to help. Thank you for those who will not turn away from "hopeless" people. You are a God who gives hope, and the gospel of Jesus is hope for a hurting world entangled in moral and personal messes. Thank you for drawing people to you in their times of deepest despair and direst disaster. Let their stories be told far and wide. Show me how I can have a part in making more of those stories possible.

▇ June 22

God, I deeply desire to see more application of biblical truth in my life and in my children's lives. Knowing your Word is necessary in order to apply it. Reading it is necessary in order to know it. Show us your truth in our experiences. A soft answer really does turn anger away (Prov. 15:1). Scripture is proven true when "pride goes before destruction" (Prov. 16:18), whether exemplified by a cocky athlete announcing that he doesn't need to practice or by a smug coworker saying, "I don't need to prepare for that meeting." When we see that the Bible is exactly on target in matters like these, increase our trust that it is true in *all* matters, all the time.

▰ June 23

Lord, grant my children the ability to enjoy being young! Guide them in their vulnerability. Protect them. Give them the courage to develop a healthy individuality and reject negative peer influence. Guide my children and my friends' children in whom they choose as their friends. When they decide not to listen to their parents, use other people or circumstances to guard their attitudes and decisions. Give my children a positive influence on others as they demonstrate values they have learned at home even without being aware of it. This is one of my most passionate desires. Hear my cries for my children's well-being. May their lives honor you!

▰ June 24

Thank you, Father, for those who have put their imaginations into delivering the gospel message through powerful movies, tracts, billboards, music videos, and other cutting-edge, clever methods of communication. The message is the same as it always has been: "Jesus Christ died so you could live!" Father, forgive us for sometimes squabbling over methods and forgetting the message. Continue to inspire your people with new ideas for conveying hope to a hopeless world. At the same time, give us more courage to continue using the oldest method there is: word of mouth.

▬ June 25

God, through your Spirit make me more like your Son, Jesus, who said, "Love your enemies, do good to those who hate you, bless those who curse you" (Luke 6:27–28). Jesus' words carry such wisdom and power! I long to see his words become truth in my life. Father, when you are given space to work in me, I am strong enough to act kindly instead of retaliate. Help me, God, to smile at people who I fear don't like me. Make me willing to talk to the person I really don't feel like talking to. Give me the grace to pray for the people who have offended me.

▬ June 26

Forgive me, Lord, for when I focus only on the outward differences between myself and a passerby: skin color, apparent socioeconomic circumstance, hairstyle, clothing, or number and location of body piercings. Lead me to see past all that and realize that the person I am looking at is essentially like me: made by you, loved by you, imperfect, and helpless in a scary universe if not sheltered by your protective hand. When I am tempted to scorn others because of their appearance or behavior, remind me that you did not scorn me. You loved me and you accepted me when I came to you as a soul in need. Help me treat others as you have treated me.

▬ June 27

I want other people to see that I've been with the Lord! May your Spirit be so active in me that people will be blessed by you when they have contact with me. Make your power and glory evident to others through me, dear God! Make me into that city on a hill that can't be hidden. I want to mirror Jesus, who is the

Light of the World. I've been told, "People will see the difference in you and will ask about the peace you have." I'm still waiting for that to happen. Please work through my life to make your power and your glory evident to others.

▰ June 28

Father, guide me to speak of your love and faithfulness not only in the safe haven of believers but also to the familiar people who usually remain strangers because I do not talk to them as they scan my groceries or style my hair. Forgive me for being so ready to assume that a stranger will be hostile toward God-talk. Satan ties my tongue; he places uncertainty in my mind about these things. Lord God, bless me with much to talk about! Fill my heart with gratitude for all you have done for me and for others to the point that, like Peter and John, I cannot keep from speaking about what I've seen and heard (see Acts 4:20).

▰ June 29

Dear Lord, a life of monastic seclusion sometimes sounds appealing, especially when life demands so much of me. But move out and become a recluse in pursuit of profound knowledge of you? Impossible! I have a family to love and serve. In the confines of my busy life, draw me into a *reasonable* amount of secluded spiritual seeking, jealously guarded, without neglect of my responsibilities. I dream of a small-scale "stimulus fast" to really clear my head and my heart. How long would it take to become emptied of all my previous assumptions? How long would I have to be away from all people and all noise to hear you when you speak? Time is an issue for me, but you are Lord of all things, including time. Speak to me, Lord, when I take the time to be quiet before you.

▆ June 30

Father of all things, your works are great! Work through my prayers. When I am plagued by guilt, lead me to pray with conviction, "There is therefore now no condemnation for those who are in Christ Jesus" (Rom. 8:1). When I or my family members are tempted to do wrong, call me to claim this promise: "God is faithful, and he will not let you be tested beyond your strength, but . . . will also provide the way out" (1 Cor. 10:13). When I feel no joy, I will repeat (and repeat and repeat), "Happy are those who live in your house" (Ps. 84:4). Then I will watch until you, Lord, cause it to be true in me. God, there is infinite power and possibility in the claiming of your Word!

july

free indeed, but not independent

So if the Son makes you free, you will be free indeed.

JOHN 8:36

I am the vine, you are the branches. Those who abide in me and I in them bear much fruit, because apart from me you can do nothing.

JOHN 15:5

■ July 1

Thank you, precious Jesus, for making me free indeed! Because of you, I am free from the fear of eternal death, free from the fear that something I do wrong can change my state of acceptability to you, free to choose self-controlled living, and free to see evidence of the fruit that such living produces. Lord, if I incorrectly view spiritual freedom as the right to do whatever I please, I am still enslaved by sin and a misunderstanding of your grace and its purpose. Give me a growing understanding of the vine-and-branch relationship I have with you.

■ July 2

Thank you, Lord Jesus, that though I am dependent on you completely, I am not a nothing. As a branch that is an integral part of the vine, I am not absorbed into the vine nor concealed by it. I thank you that our co-abiding does not negate my individuality, making me into some kind of brainless shell. I am not a marionette! Thank you for what is unique about me. Help me use my special gifts, abilities, and personality traits to honor you as I seek with all my heart to become more like you.

■ July 3

Lord Jesus, Scripture records that you said your purpose on earth was to bring good news, to proclaim release to the captives, and to free the oppressed (Luke 4:17–21). I am so grateful that this good news continues to be told today. As former captives now released, we are free to become our best selves in you. Thank you that as the vine you do not choke out our lives or our individuality. Let us not be choking branches to one another, either, as we work to announce your Good News. As believers not subject to the detail of the Old Testament law, help us not to try to impose our own particular style of "churchianity" on others.

▰ July 4

Political freedom is the obvious kind of freedom to think about today; thank you, dear God, for the long years of freedom this country has known. Thank you for all who have sacrificed in different ways to protect our freedom. Thank you also that the freedom I have in you is mine no matter what happens in national government or world politics. Lord, I need freedom in my mind and heart from selfishness, anger, ego, stubbornness, and other tendencies that infringe on the freedom spoken of in John 8:36, "So if the Son makes you free, you will be free indeed."

▰ July 5

Heavenly Father, many of the opportunities afforded in the land of the free and the home of the brave lead to a dangerous sense of self-sufficiency. Forgive me for when I've basked in a self-satisfied view of how much I have achieved. Much opportunity to give you credit and to call on your wisdom and power has been lost along the way. Renew my passion to have my life inextricably meshed with the Holy Spirit! In spite of the knowledge of all I can do as a capable woman with lots of irons in the fire, never let me lose sight of my utter dependence on you for every strength and ability.

▰ July 6

Lord Jesus, seldom do I find myself in mortal danger from physical perils like fire or flood, but too often do mental and emotional threats assail me. Let me learn to depend on your power to beat back those threats just as the disciples called on you during the perilous storm you later calmed. Fear and worry over what the future may bring is a real peril to me. Calm that storm within me, I pray, and give me a true inward and outward peace because of the assurance that you will not forsake me no matter what may happen in this world.

▰ July 7

Lord God, some might say that you devised a grand schedule eons ago, pushed the "go" button, and have been watching from a distance ever since. But I believe the very universe depends *daily* on your divine direction. In the same way a house depends on its foundation every day, not just some of the time, I depend on you every day as the source and basis of my existence. In the same way an aircraft depends on its guidance instrumentation for every flight, not just certain flights, I depend on you for guidance to keep me from crashing, every day, 100 percent of the time.

▰ July 8

Thank you, God, for freedom from cumbersome rules and regulations too detailed and numerous to comply with. Thank you for Jesus' summary of the law: love the Lord your God with all your being, and love your neighbor the way you love yourself (see Mark 12:30–31). Help us move from pretty words to real love in practice! How much I want my children to see that I really do consider someone else's present need important enough for me to inconvenience myself by rearranging my schedule or giving up altogether something I had planned to do. Lord, unless I live that way, much of what I say to my children will be hypocritical.

▰ July 9

Lord, make me free indeed to worship without allowing anyone to dictate how I should worship. Reveal to me what is true and acceptable worship in *your* eyes, not others'. Set me free from longtime mistaken assumptions; from gossip and complaining; from self-centeredness in how I use my resources; and from a self-important view that others are not really worth my notice. If I view someone as a "loser," a nonentity, I am a poor representative of you. That is not how you love; that is not part of the image you created me to reflect! How I conduct myself all week in matters like these is really my true worship.

▰ July 10

Free me, dear Lord, from the subtle addiction of shopping. Let me not be careless or wasteful in handling money. Guide me to exemplify and to teach to my children the freedom that comes from a biblical approach to financial stewardship. True, I can't put my ultimate trust in riches, but that should not be an excuse for fiscal ignorance. Scripture shows that you expect people to use money cleverly, both for survival and for ministry. Let me be appropriately conscious of what a dollar can do and what it can't do so that I will assign neither too little nor too great an importance to monetary resources.

▰ July 11

Lord, I am dependent on you for guidance so that I don't weaken in my convictions and slowly inch toward acceptance of what once made me recoil. Forgive me, heavenly Father, for the times I've asked your guidance, recognized what was right or best to do, and then proceeded to do something else because it was what I wanted to do in the first place. Forgive me for behaving that way even after I have begged and begged you for "clear" answers to complex problems. Knowing that sincere and frequent prayer is the most obvious key to understanding your voice clearly, may I make that my life's habit.

▬ July 12

Scripture uses a "potter and clay" analogy to picture your role as a Creator who shapes and molds us when we trust in you. But cultural messages insist that I not let myself be molded by anyone or anything. Culture tells me to break molds and be myself. The idea of being molded by any outside source creates defiance and resistance in me. How much I'd have to trust, respect, and admire someone to let myself be molded by that person. Christ Jesus, you are the one I need to be imitating. Make me more like you.

▬ July 13

Scripture teaches servant leadership (Matt. 20:27) and humility as a prerequisite for exaltation (Luke 14:7–11; James 4:10). Thank you, God, for those who lead by serving rather than lording it over their subordinates. Help me remember that I am in leadership positions in many situations, even when I am not the teacher or the chairperson. It may be at the dinner table, in my peer group, or in line at a crowded store. In dependence on you, Lord, let me choose humility even when I think I have the verbal ability and the so-called right to tell someone off or take my agenda right to the top no matter who else is waiting.

▰ July 14

To live! To be free, really free! These drives have not changed since the human race began, though the settings and the particulars have evolved and repeated. Lord, I find comfort in the fact that the basic elements of human living have not changed; that's why Scripture recorded centuries ago speaks right to our situations today. Speak to us through the Bible in everything that it says. It teaches that the only way to be really free is to voluntarily enslave ourselves to righteousness and to Christ (Rom. 6:18, 20; 1 Cor. 7:22). If we are skeptical of this, open our eyes and our hearts to the truth.

▰ July 15

Father, I want to pray for the "right" things, but underneath my sincerity is lurking a deep-down desire that you will see things my way. Free me from this stubborn insistence on retaining some control! Losing my life for your sake is not keeping control. To be like Christ is to say, "Not my will, but yours be done." Give me the submission to wrap all of my prayer requests in the desire that you will bring your will into my life and the lives of those I pray for so that our lives will reflect your glory.

▰ July 16

Help me see that it is not weakness but wisdom to relinquish control to you, loving God! Apart from you I can do nothing, though I fool myself into believing I am doing a lot. It is not weakness, Lord, to admit to being weak! It is weakness, rather, to pretend to be "basically okay" even when my weaknesses stick out all over, marring my marriage and other relationships and my efforts to succeed. When I am weak and recognize that I am weak, then I am in a position to be stronger than ever in Christ (2 Cor. 12:9–10). Let me speak gladly of how you minister to me in my weaknesses when I depend on you.

■ July 17

Thank you, heavenly Father, for the influence of godly parents who approach big and small matters with prayer and faith rather than reserving all talk of God and the Bible for a church setting. Help me be the one who reads a Bible story like David and Goliath and reminds my husband and children that our God still helps underdogs slay giants of all kinds. Thank you for the times you have led me through a giant challenge, comforted me through a giant sorrow, and saved me from a giant calamity. Thank you for taking care of your people. Help us depend on you more.

■ July 18

"Freedom 101: Accepting My Accountability to God." Sign me up, dear Lord! Front-row desk with lots of note paper. In a culture that emphasizes individual achievement, personal power, and spiritualism in every form from meditation to witchcraft, the starting point is acknowledging your supremacy and your unique-ness as the one true God. This is the clear message you have been revealing since the time of Moses—no, of Adam! You are God. I am dependent on you for my physical survival and my spiritual destiny. It can't get any plainer than that, can it?

■ July 19

"Freedom 201: Casting All My Cares upon Him." A follow-up course I definitely need! Lord Jesus, you said to your disciples,

"I do not call you servants any longer . . . but I have called you friends" (John 15:15). Thank you that once a person has received you as Savior, a personal relationship—a friendship—can develop. Lord, one of the best qualities a friend can have is a listening ear, and I believe that is why you have invited us to cast our cares upon you (1 Peter 5:7). Thank you for being a Lord who is not only master but also friend.

■ July 20

Lord, I am dependent on you for something extremely basic: my sense of personal worth. My ability to feel good about who I am does not have to depend on how good I think others feel about me! I can feel good about who I am because you made and love the person I am. Help me stay absolutely convinced of that, and use me to help others understand it about themselves. Prompt me more often to affirm others verbally, both in their presence and in their absence. We all need regular affirmation of the kind that is true to Scripture. We do not need a false sense of self-worth that comes from others' flattery or from our own pep talks in front of the mirror.

■ July 21

God, remind me that today I can't ride on the coattails of anything I did successfully yesterday, like keeping my patience with my children. I have to depend on your strength and your power, invoked through prayer each day; otherwise, yesterday's success goes right into the trash can when I fail on the same issue today. I've seen this so many times; I've made so many returns to the same old regrettable thought or speech habits. I want to experience success, maturing, and visible-at-the-time progress so that I can gain ground instead of always slipping back just as far as I've progressed.

▰ July 22

Romans 12:1–2 speaks of being transformed instead of being conformed to this world, and I see from the tracks of my life that without transformation I will be stuck in continual fluctuation, developing no substantial spiritual maturity. Without transformation I will stay a slave to inconsistency. Though I can learn to be more deliberate about studying and learning of you, Father, transformation is not something I can make happen. You have to do that. Thank you for being on the job and working in me even when I am not aware of it. You have promised not to walk away from the good work you have begun in me (Phil. 1:6). Thank you for that promise!

▰ July 23

I want to be transformed, Lord Jesus, so that I don't resist your work in my heart and mind. If I felt I was being led along on a restrictive leash, I might be inclined to chew through the leash and run away. My choice to live according to your spiritual laws, to live with discipline, sets me free from the negative results of unrestrained actions. The value of discipline is plainly visible in money management and time management. Make me as excited over results from spiritual discipline as I am over a CD maturing at the bank or over completing a project and being able to go on vacation as a result.

▰ July 24

Lord God, I want the fruit my life produces to be undeniable evidence that you are the vine and I am a branch. I want this fruit to look like fruit of the kind of tree I say I am. Prevent me from being a Christian who talks about peace but worries all the time; who talks about joy but spends a lot of time dejected; who talks about love but criticizes and scorns other people constantly; who talks about patience and kindness but loses her temper and uses excessive sarcasm; who talks about gentleness but displays harshness; and who talks about self-control and discipline but chooses the easy-at-the-moment path more often than not.

■ July 25

Thank you, God, for the benefit gained by a lifelong habit of spending at least one hour each week in public worship, listening to truth from the Bible drawn out and illustrated by a speaker you have called to a preaching ministry. Bring more people to the point where they crave to be fed spiritually in a church environment. Nothing else in the diet offered by culture can substitute for that kind of spiritual nutrition. There is strength in the family of faith! That's why you said, "I am the vine; you are the *branches*" (John 15:5). A plant would be abnormal with only one branch. Draw the lone believer and the seeker into a company of other believers who can provide support and encouragement.

■ July 26

Lord, only in dependence on you and the power of your Word can I overcome the natural human tendency to choose self-promotion over humility. "Because I can" has become the popular chant. It proclaims, "I take precedence. I matter more than you do." Much of the marketing climate in business tries to capitalize on that attitude. In me, Father, make "because I can" apply more to humility than to self-promotion. Make me less interested in mowing others down verbally and mentally. Teach me to choose to stay in the background sometimes *because I can*—I do not need the spotlight because I know I am important to you!

▄ July 27

Father, it's tempting to focus only on Bible verses that make me feel good. The verse about the vine and branches (John 15:5) is one of those. But it is followed by, "Whoever does not abide in me is thrown away like a branch and withers; such branches are gathered, thrown into the fire, and burned" (John 15:6). Scripture is not all rosy and cozy! Fact: You are God and you are in charge. Fact: Each person has a choice to abide by your ways and live or defy you and die. Give me the courage to ask the most important people in my life which choice they have made.

▄ July 28

Lord, I face a fine line between being down on myself and assessing my weaknesses in an honest and constructive way. I know I have weaknesses; everyone has them. Make me understanding and forgiving when it comes to weaknesses, both others' and my own, but prevent me from being so lenient with myself that I continually dismiss or excuse my faults by saying, "This is just my personality; I can't help it." Thank you, O Father, for loving me enough to accept me in spite of my weaknesses, and thank you for loving me enough not to leave me as I am but to nudge me toward improvement.

▄ July 29

John 16:12 reads, "I still have many things to say to you, but you cannot bear them now." I am touched by the gentleness and understanding in those words, Lord Jesus. You have an obvious love and compassion for human beings, Lord, or else you would not care for us in a manner that takes into account the way we are made and the needs we have. You could make us into puppets, but you don't.

You could transform us at a rate that would shock our systems and leave us completely bewildered, but you don't. Thank you for taking the time to deal with us on a schedule we can bear.

▄ July 30

Lord, I am more conscious of my dependence on you as I age and as the world seems to grow more dangerous. I realize that the form I move around in is a weak, mortal, temporary body. Only as you enable it will it continue to do what I need it to do. Death will come; I can't ignore that fact, but I must not dwell on it so much that I forget to live. Father, I have a deep heart-knowledge of your love and protection; I need a more conscious head-knowledge of that to tread without fear in a world where violent and tragic things occur every day. Send me thoughts of peace and comfort!

▄ July 31

Lord, I feel ready for summer heat to change into autumn cool, but it's not time for that yet. Sometimes I feel very ready for other unsatisfactory things to change, but apparently your timetable is different from mine. And, Lord, other things are just fine with me the way they are, but change comes. Fun events end. Dear friends move away. Children grow up. Green fields become housing developments. Pets die. People die. Change hurts, Lord! Help me depend on you as the one constant in my life. You are my comfort. Only in you can I find freedom from the fear of change. Only when I am abiding in you will it even occur to me to seek in you the comfort I need.

august

so laughter's not lost

Likewise all to whom God gives wealth and possessions and whom he enables to enjoy them, and to accept their lot and find enjoyment in their toil—this is the gift of God. For they will scarcely brood over the days of their lives, because God keeps them occupied with the joy of their hearts.

ECCLESIASTES 5:19–20

a gentle suggestion

See, as you reach for success you can measure,
That life is not slain on the altar of thriving.
Sad if in gaining you're robbed of the pleasure
Of listening and seeing and caring and giving.

Work, yet uncover the secrets of leisure
So laughter's not lost for the sake of your striving.
Smile as you ponder the people you treasure,
And then you may find you get more out of living.

■ August 1

Dear God, your Word is so full of promises, far more in number than I take hold of in my own life. Give me the faith to seek your promises more and to pray until I see them proved in my circumstances. Give me the gifts described in Ecclesiastes 5:19–20. Enjoyment in my toil? Enjoyment in something that sounds synonymous with tedium, sweat, and stress? That sounds contradictory! But in your wisdom you created us to need work. Give me joy in my daily toil, whatever it may be. Oh, how greatly this world needs more people occupied with the joy, rather than the unfulfilled desires, of their hearts!

■ August 2

Lord, I don't think they had a word in Bible times for "stress," but they experienced it: "My soul is troubled within me," "grieved," "afraid," "mourn," "weep," "sorrowful." Lord, I thank you for being the one who can turn weeping into laughing and mourning into dancing. You care about worried, stressed, grieving, and frustrated individuals. You comfort us, so much of the time without our realizing you are doing that. You give us friends we can unload our frustrations on and counselors, pastors, and doctors to help us with what we cannot solve on our own. Thank you for what you have provided for our well-being.

■ August 3

Thank you, wonderful Father, for the fact that the word *stress* is so close alphabetically to *strength*. If we're looking at Bible reference materials for mentions of stress, maybe we'll stop at "strength" instead. When stress is my enemy, give me strength. "Strengthen me according to your word" (Ps. 119:28),

117

not according to selfish plans I might have for the moment or the long term. If I don't find strength to complete my daily to-do list, maybe my to-do list isn't according to your Word. I want it to be, Lord. Help me learn more of your Word so I will know what "according to it" really means in my choices and activities.

■ August 4

I don't know if I could count the number of times I laugh in a day, but it might be revealing to try. Thank you, Lord, for the gift of laughter. The older I get, the more I see laughter as a gift, because I can't necessarily count on it showing up in the course of a normal day. "A cheerful heart is a good medicine" (Prov. 17:22); oh, yes, Lord, and I need bigger doses of that medicine than ever before. Give me more laughter, I pray—laughter not at other people's misfortunes nor at off-color jokes. Open my eyes to the wholesome humor that makes my heart cheerful.

■ August 5

Remind us, Father, to get things in the right order. To get and keep more laughter in our lives, first we have to be serious about certain things. If we take school and work seriously, we can laugh with pleasure at graduation or promotion. A responsible start can give us more to laugh about in the end. Having a laughter-first or a laughter-only approach to life can lead to less laughter, more stress, less forgiveness, and less meaning in relationships. Lord, help us pull and build into our lives more of what brings lasting laughter.

■ August 6

Lord, somehow we like to think we are smarter than our predecessors, so we disdain certain spiritual terminology as outdated jargon. We modernize the words, making sin and temptation sound like things to be sought after instead of avoided. A dessert is "sinfully delicious." "Temptation" is a marketing tactic rather than a spiritual battle. Sin and temptation are just as serious now as always, and they are based on the same weaknesses people have always had, including greed, selfishness, sexual curiosity, and cowardice that results in joining a pack with no good purpose. Temptation leads to trouble when we give in to it but to joy when we withstand and overcome it. So, I pray, lead us not into temptation, and deliver us from evil.

■ August 7

Forgive me, Lord God, for when I have sat in church with a spirit of criticism instead of worship. It is almost impossible not to notice the occasional musical mess-up or the "so-so" sermon delivery. People who sing and speak are only human, and so are the ones who sit in the congregation listening. Help me understand the human factor in church things, then receive feeding and spiritual healing because of the God factor! I do not come to church to be entertained but to praise, to listen, to learn, and to be changed. I do not serve behind the scenes to earn recognition but to give of my gifts with humility and joy.

■ August 8

Dear Lord, Scripture instructs us to pray for our enemies. Prompt me to do that, and also to quit seeing so many people as my enemies, consciously or subconsciously. Father, when there

119

is conflict in the home, including the petty mouthing-offs and the mutterings of ugly things behind people's backs as they leave the room, I am behaving as if a loved one is my enemy. Give me the strength to choose *not* to have the last word and prove I'm right.

▬ August 9

Lord, some would sneer at the idea of enjoying their toil and being occupied with the joy of their hearts (Eccles. 5:19–20), because they are occupied with headaches and heartaches on the job—and at home, which affect them at work. Comfort and encourage those who can barely make themselves return daily to their work, Lord. Impossible? Unlikely? Too general? But if not you, then to whom am I supposed to tell my "impossible," unlikely, and sweeping requests? You, who can create mountains and move them, can encourage people who are unhappy in their work. God, make your presence known to people today in offices, factories, stores, classrooms, and construction sites.

▬ August 10

Father God, sometimes it's hard to smile as I ponder the people I treasure when they spill things on the carpet, leave dirty clothes all over the place, argue over the stupidest things, and generally get on my nerves! Lord, I get on their nerves, too. I behave stupidly, too. Help each of us to learn more patience, tolerance, and appreciation. When my husband annoys me, recall to me all his good qualities that make me thankful to have him as my mate. When my mind calls my beloved child "a pain" or "a trial," help me be loving through that "unlovable" moment.

■ August 11

Thank you, God, for friends who almost always have a smile for me. I'm sure they don't feel happy "24-7," but I appreciate their ability to help me feel cheerful with their positive attitude. That's a gift, Lord, straight from you. I may not have that gift myself, but I don't want my face to shout, "Downcast!" When I am serious and contemplative, I am exercising a different gift from you. But if my serious face looks troubled to others, give me words to convey that peace and joy are underneath, because they are, thanks entirely to you!

■ August 12

Whatever news the day brings, heavenly Father, give me joy in my heart—joy that the world did not give me and that the world cannot take away. If the news of the day is bad, let me pray for your mercy and healing, trusting that you will hear and sustain all who hurt even though the "feeling better" cannot always happen immediately. If the news is good, let me celebrate it, even if simply by phoning a friend or parent. And, Lord, please forgive me for not recognizing so much good news all around, every day: acts of love and integrity; destinations reached without mishap; children who were not neglected; and life conducted with order, not chaos.

■ August 13

Lord, all of my wealth comes from you. And I don't mean just tangibles like money, house, car, food, and clothing. My definition of wealth must include *all* that makes life rich and rewarding: friends, smiles, hugs, music, health, ice cream, sunsets, and so much more. Let me define possessions not only as the physical items I own but also as intangibles like peace of mind, self-respect, and faith. Although they can be elusive, these are some of my most precious possessions. Thank you for the wealth no person can steal and no disaster can destroy. I will stand a better chance of keeping joy and laughter in my life if most of my treasure is internal.

▰ August 14

Dear Lord, make us realize once again that there is more pleasure in commenting on what is right than in complaining about what is wrong! A TV character once said, "Have you noticed that the temperature in this room is absolutely perfect?" That caught my ear. *That's an odd remark,* I thought. It should not be so odd! And there is that absurd but indicting old joke about the child who never spoke a word until age seven, and then only to complain about the food because "up until now, everything's been okay!" Give us wisdom in our speech. Lead us to point out at least *one* right thing for every uncomfortable and unacceptable thing it is necessary to comment on.

▰ August 15

Lord, some people can pretty much be counted on to gripe about particular issues when I see them. Give me the grace not to join in (or to gripe back). I've determined that I don't want to turn into a complaining old woman, but it would be very easy to do that. Stop me, please! Make me thankful when only one knee hurts rather than both. Make me thankful that only one of my children is difficult to rouse on school mornings. Make me joyful over a dishwasher that holds *most* of my dishes even if it won't hold all of them. And, when I am frustrated over someone's behavior, make me joyful about the persons whose company I really enjoy. I have so much to be thankful for! Forgive me for complaining.

▬ August 16

Dear God, help me as a parent not only to correct my children but to pray that they will learn from their mistakes and continue their lives with restored joy and more confidence that they can make good choices. That's exactly the kind of spiritual parenting I boldly expect from you; I should not neglect the similar nurture of the precious children you have given to me. Your power is great enough to forgive sin. It is great enough to prevent sin, too. Help us forgive, learn, and go on with joy. Satan's greatest success is in our failure to do that.

▬ August 17

O God, give me the grace to be joyful about prayers you have answered! Too often I say "thank you" once (if at all), and it's on to the next request on *my list*. Thank you for when I have seen clear indication of progress in a situation I prayed about and have recognized that progress to be your work. Certainly you have worked behind the scenes, too, before I ever began to pray. You know what I need before I ask, loving Father (Matt. 6:8). Thank you for being a wonderful counselor and advocate! Knowing this makes it much easier for me to be occupied with joy instead of worry.

▬ August 18

Lord, I trust that my prayers make a difference in the lives of people whose needs I've become aware of. I believe it matters that

I stop to pray the moment my heart is touched and bothered by national news or personal phone calls. I believe my prayers make an important difference in friends' and strangers' lives, even if I pray about a situation only once. I am thankful that you hear a one-time prayer. I am also thankful that you call me to pray again and again for certain situations.

■ August 19

Thank you, God, for good and sweet and pleasing things that seldom fail to catch my eye and make me smile: cute puppies, beautiful little children, amusing snapshots, raindrop patterns on the car window, a perfect leaf, a crescent moon in an autumn sky. Thank you for the purpose and perfection in what you have created and ordained. It's easy to lose sight of that when so much is wrong and *stays* wrong. Please help me change the wrong that I can change, leave the rest to you, and keep noticing, with joy, the cute puppies and the raindrop patterns on the car windows.

■ August 20

Lord, patience is an endangered virtue in this "never say wait" culture. Cause patience to be a character strength in me, and use it as an antidote for stress. I'd like to be able to sit in my car for six minutes before the bank opens and not consider it wasted time. I need to be able to wait months when that letter or hoped-for circumstance does not come without being unappreciative of all else that's good in my life. I want to be able to wait years for goals to be achieved—because of patience. Patience is a fruit of the Holy Spirit (Gal. 5:22). Give me patience as proof that your Spirit is working in me.

■ August 21

"I was glad when they said to me, 'Let us go to the house of the Lord!'" (Ps. 122:1). Lord, I *am* glad to worship in your house! Psalm 27:6 speaks of offering sacrifices in your tent with shouts of joy. My sacrifices are not like ancient ones: no animals, no bags of meal or spices. My sacrifice might be a tithe of money that could have purchased the latest home entertainment gizmo. It might be getting dirty from baby formula in the nursery or not going out Saturday night because a Sunday school lesson needed polishing. Give me joy about these sacrifices—joy because I am able to offer them to a God I love.

■ August 22

Father, my speech is a good indication of whether strength or stress, faith or defeat, is in control. Give me words of hope, not helplessness! I don't want to say in frustration, "You're going to make us late again." I'd rather be heard saying, "Let's help each other get ready so we can be on time and in a good mood." Not "He's going to end up just like his no-account father," but "He's had a bad start, but God can turn him around if we pray faithfully and try to help all we can." Not "You're the messiest eater I have ever seen!" but "Sweetheart, we are going to find a way to help you eat with fewer spills."

■ August 23

When my family and I need to snap out of our dull though hectic routine, show us something we've seen or accomplished that we can call special and celebrate in a fun way. Give me some extra creativity in my role as wife and in my role as mother. Too often I lump the two roles together. Show me how to be better at each, seeing wisely how each affects the other. Prompt me to make a bigger deal out of workday successes, high test grades, and good medical reports. Certainly it's simpler (and sometimes less tiring) to skip the celebration, but it's also less memorable and less fulfilling. Help us find more things to celebrate—not just about what we achieve, but about ourselves, too.

■ August 24

As school terms are beginning this time of year, loving God, I pray for safety and positive learning experiences. I pray that teachers and administrators will be energized and not burned out. Call out strong adult and student leaders in our schools. And when I feel impatient because a school bus slows me down on the highway, remind me that a child on that bus may become a doctor, pastor, merchant, or teacher who helps me or my children one day. O Lord, I *must* look and think and pray beyond the present moment. Help me act on that conviction more and more as you lead me to a clearly *eternal* perspective on life.

■ August 25

Caution us through your Spirit's voice, O Lord, when we find ourselves laughing at the surface humor in things that warrant a closer look. Some "funny" ads and TV shows present characters with excessively in-your-face attitudes. "Cool" kids get the better of adults, and everyone laughs. Help us see, and effectively point out to our children, what is being communicated. Make us aware of the agendas that often lurk behind the humor, and let us discuss the values being portrayed and promoted through comedy. Give us clean laughter, too, from sources we can trust.

▰ August 26

Father, football season is upon us, at all levels from elementary to professional. It's fun, it's pageantry, and it's big business. Like many other things, it brings out the best in some and the worst in others. When we participate in football as fans or as parents of players, band members, and cheerleaders, guard us against unkindness. Protect those who play and those who travel with their teams. Guide coaches and sponsors to lead by example and build character in others and in themselves. Lord, tell us again and again that all talent, athletic and otherwise, comes from you. And, Lord, where there is friction between family members over an obsession with football, I pray for resolution.

▰ August 27

Proverbs 10:23 assures, "Doing wrong is like sport to a fool, but wise conduct is pleasure to a person of understanding." Tell that to those who are convinced that being a Christian takes all the fun out of life, God! Your Word is so wise, yet such a stumbling block when we are too blind to see the truth. Wise conduct is a *pleasure?* Absolutely. Oh, give us understanding of something so simple but so foreign to our human nature! Lead us to pray with dedication and passion for those who are playing around with wrongdoing. Show us when "those" are us. Give us maturity as believers, dear Lord. Give us tremendous pleasure in conducting ourselves wisely.

▰ August 28

God, thank you for the joy of seeing children succeed. Let me never be jealous of any young and healthy person who still has opportunities I may never have again. I find it easy to envy their energy, physical mobility, and freedom. But let me process that envy in a nondestructive way. Help me take pleasure in *their* pleasure. Lead me to encourage young people to make the most of their abilities while conducting themselves wisely. Raise up a new generation who will take matters of faith and eternity very seriously! Bless our young people, O God! Make them strong, wise, and able to conquer any obstacle in your name.

■August 29

Lord God, I take great pleasure in many things: music, reading, creating with my hands, learning, worshiping, interacting with others, solving problems, and much more. I love to be challenged intellectually, and I love to laugh at subtle humor and at slapstick. But laughter goes only so far. It can't erase crime, disease, and sorrow. These things deeply trouble and sadden me, Lord, sometimes to the point that, like the apostle Paul, I long to be away from the body so I can be at home with you (2 Cor. 5:8). Sustain me with a permanent joy through the things of this world that cannot be laughed away.

■August 30

Precious Savior, bring me to my private altar of prayer more often without a written or mental list of prayer requests, without a busy day's agenda on the tip of my tongue, and without one eye on the clock. Lord, tell me your agenda as I pray. Make me holier as I fall before you without words. Make me more interested in your will than in my own words and wishes. Make me aware of how things really are in the physical world I can see and in the spiritual realm I cannot see. And when I arise to go on with life's chores, let me be a more confident and joyful person than I was when I knelt.

▰ August 31

Psalm 11:7 reads, "For the LORD is righteous; he loves righteous deeds; the upright shall behold his face." Because you have made me righteous through your Son, Jesus, I shall behold your face, Lord! When laughter eludes me and *joy* is a word I leave at church, remind me that I shall behold your face! When toil is a pain and fatigue is my constant companion, whisper to me, "You shall behold my face!" Thank you, God, for this promise. I want to trust it. Cause it to make my life happier here and now. Give me your Word in my heart as I read it with my eyes. Occupy me with joy, precious Lord!

september

i'm not superwoman!

Help, O LORD . . .

PSALM 12:1

i'm not superwoman

As much as I would like to be Superwoman, I can't be.
I am miles from being Superwoman.
Superwoman's house wouldn't be this dirty.
Superwoman's house wouldn't be dirty at all.
Superwoman's house wouldn't have a Macy's bag lying on the
    kitchen floor, from a purchase made days ago.

Superwoman would never forget her grandmother's birthday
    or be late for work
        or allow one of the children to spill a strawberry milkshake
    in Dad's company car.
She would never have
    overdue books from the library or
    overdue movies from the video store or
    a bad hair day.
She would never misplace
    her glasses
    her keys
    or her entire purse.
(Superwoman would never *wear* glasses.)

Superwoman would never make a false start
    into a four-way-stop intersection

or graze another car in the supermarket parking lot.
And Superwoman would *never* lock her keys in the trunk.

Superwoman would always eat the right foods
and get enough rest.
Her fingernails and toenails would always be neatly painted.
The same color.
Superwoman would be either the perfect
"Donna Reed" homemaker
or the perfect, got-it-all-together career woman.
She would never feel like
an ineffective compromise between the two.
Superwoman would have a clear sense of purpose
instead of feeling pulled in many different directions.

Superwoman would SAVE THE WORLD!
She would never be afraid of it.

Superwoman would never cry.

Superwoman would never wait two months
to balance the checkbook.
Superwoman's ice trays would never stay empty.
Superwoman's bed would be made every day. Early in the day.
Very early in the day.
Superwoman would never burn a grilled cheese sandwich
because she got engrossed in emptying the dishwasher.
Superwoman would be a soprano soloist, not an adequate alto
in the choir's second row.

Superwoman would never say stupid things that embarrass her.
She would never hurt a friend's feelings thoughtlessly.
She would never lose her temper.
Superwoman would never feel sorry for herself.

And Superwoman would have no need of God.

Superwoman is not real, because all real people
   have need of God.
I am real.
Real vulnerable. Real concerned.
   Real happy. Real sad. Real needy.

I'm not Superwoman!
Superwoman does not *exist*.

But super women do.

A super woman never focuses only on her failings,
   but recognizes her unique abilities and celebrates them.
A super woman remembers to take note of
   and take heart in
      all that she does right.

A super woman pauses
   in the midst of the mundane and the monotonous
      to remember
      the perfect golden-brown meringue
      on that last chocolate pie
      (and how the friends who shared it raved about it);
   to reflect
      on major and minor successes in life which are such
      standard performance they tend not to stand out
      or be appreciated as they really should;
   to realize
      the world needs altos as well as sopranos.

A super woman fights feelings of dejection
   by reminding herself of all the

birthdays remembered
school projects helped with
lost objects found
dresses sewn
piano lessons given
reports written
hugs shared
meals prepared
deadlines met
sorrows consoled
biscuits rolled
shoes tied
new recipes tried
coworkers helped
lessons learned
money earned
calls returned
and grilled cheese sandwiches not burned.

A super woman acknowledges to herself
the many gifts and abilities she brings
to her family
to her work
to her world.
She remembers that each gift and each ability
comes from God and can be used to honor him.
Above all, she finds her personal worth in God's perfect love
and sees the futility of trying to achieve or prove worth
through her own accomplishments.

There is no Superwoman.
But there are a great many *super women*.

And I am one of them.

■September 1

Help, Lord! I read Luke 12:48 and come away thinking, *This is the overachiever's byword, the workaholic's creed:* "From everyone to whom much has been given, much will be required." I long to do what you require, but I can't do everything. I'm not Superwoman! Help me not to labor under the assumption that something is required by you when in truth it's just something I'm demanding from myself. I don't want guilty feelings to make me overextend myself, but I also don't want to miss the joy of giving. Show me plainly what you require, please, as I study and try to obey your teachings.

■September 2

Savior God, my busy life is full of memory aids: grocery lists, to-do lists, calendars, address books. I use a computer to capture recipes and other helpful things. I need to keep some record of my praying, too. Without a guide, how could I possibly expect to remember the names of all the people I should pray for and have been asked by others to pray for? Father, I believe that when I take prayer seriously enough to keep a record of how I have prayed and how you have answered, I will begin to understand how seriously you take my prayers! When I have prayed and then forgotten what I prayed, I surely have failed to recognize answers when you gave them and therefore have not thanked you. Please forgive me.

■September 3

Lord God, you have saved me from my sin. Today, please save me from myself. Save me from the things I frequently struggle with. Save me from hurting myself (and not just physically), embarrassing myself, and outsmarting myself. God, you reign, but not as one too high and mighty to involve yourself in my life. You not only reign, but govern—"hands on," not aloof like one who merely signs laws and makes grand speeches. You roll up your sleeves and work. You help me, not as a distant and careful-not-to-get-too-personally-involved case worker, but as one who loves. I am so thankful you are that kind of God!

▬ September 4

Scripture warns against the acquisition of riches for their own sake, dear Father. Although owning any particular thing may not be a sin, I have done wrong if I have stolen from you the tithe of my income in order to purchase it. Furthermore, if I speed to my next appointment in a nice SUV, treating other drivers rudely or dangerously, I have not pleased you. If you have blessed me with the means to have manicures, designer clothes, or even a second home, I am obligated to honor you through those luxuries (Prov. 3:9–10). Lead me, Lord, to receive your blessings gratefully, to return the tithe, to share generously, to acquire useful things in moderation, and to use every possession to serve you in some way.

▬ September 5

Thank you, God, for a job and the ability to perform it. Thank you for those who pour into their work every day the skills and ingenuity you have given them. Bless the ones who are unhappy in their work, those who are looking for work, and those who are unable to work. Guide individuals to find identity not in how they earn a living but in your purpose for their lives. Bless those who needed a day of rest today but won't get one because they had to be at work. And, loving Lord, help those who find it more pleasant to be at work than to be in their own homes.

September 6

Father, as I deal daily with skin care, hair care, clothing, accessories, and diet, remind me of what Proverbs 11:22 says: "Like a gold ring in a pig's snout is a beautiful woman without good sense." Give me beauty that is not just skin deep. I want to be known and remembered as a woman who had "Proverbs 31" beauty. That Proverbs 31 woman was a real *super woman.* Her life honored and promoted her husband. She worked from predawn until long after dark to support her family, and always with wisdom and kindness. Help me, Lord, to be more like that!

September 7

Holy God, I desire to know more of your Word, but memorizing does not come as easily as it did when I was younger. Nevertheless, help me read, reread, and establish concepts in my mind even if I can't always quote word for word. And help me find practical applications of Scripture, because I know that if I do, it will make what I have read take hold. Words are just words until they get off the page and into an experience. Make Scripture more of a treasure to me than it now is! Make my faith relevant to everything I do, not something I pull out only on certain days or only with certain people.

September 8

Savior, I have grand notions of spending hours a day in prayer for relatives, friends, colleagues, neighbors, ministers, doctors, politicians, and famous people who are featured on magazine covers. Help me not to be frustrated when I don't have *hours* to devote to prayer. Make me faithful and passionate when I pray. Help me to schedule prayer without it being mechanical. Let me pray spontaneously without being flippant. Thank you for hearing the cries of my heart whether they are uttered in eloquence or in plain old broken English. Prayer is an offering of part of my day to you. Forgive me for the times I've withheld that offering.

▰ September 9

Dear Lord, today let me be an astute observer of what's really going on around me, rather than just being a participant in the mass movement or being swept along by the same old currents of learned behavior, personal routine, and cultural persuasion. Let me see people as they are and hear what their conversation tells about their needs and priorities—not so I can be a spiritual know-it-all, but so I can be a more sensitive coworker, a better friend, and a more effective wife and mother. So I can empathize and be of help. So I can be more like you.

▰ September 10

My Helper, you know how much I dread being around You-Know-Who. I pray that the next encounter will not be so bad. Often, reality is not as bad as dread would have me think, but still the dread works on me. And it's not as if this particular problem is something I could confront and resolve. It's just an ongoing ill-at-ease feeling with no logical cause. If this is a "thorn in the flesh" like the one the apostle Paul prayed you would remove from him, please provide the strength I need to cope with it. Assure me that your grace is sufficient.

▄ September 11

On this significant anniversary date, many prayers will go up for our nation and for the many hurt directly and indirectly by the terrorist attacks of September 11, 2001. I echo those prayers, Lord, and I deeply long for the people of this nation to act in a manner consistent with the "God bless America" talk that erupted in the wake of those attacks. I also pray, Lord, that we will learn the value and necessity of seeking you as passionately in peacetime and prosperity as we do in crisis! Bless us, Lord, by correcting our ways. May we desire to please you more than we desire to please ourselves.

▄ September 12

Please help me, Lord, to *really* believe and practice what I'm always saying I believe—for example, that I trust in you supremely and not in job security, 401(k), family, friends, community, or nation. I want to belong to a nation "whose God is the LORD," because such a nation is blessed, according to the Bible (Ps. 33:12). Let me not trust in chariots or horses, as some did in Old Testament days, but in the Lord my God. Let me not trust in a strong military, a strong government, or a strong economy. Support them, yes. Be thankful for them, absolutely. But place my ultimate sense of security in them? No. Only in you.

▄ September 13

Lord, I feel locked into an unbreakable pattern of overactivity—home maintenance, kids' life maintenance, work, church, a bit of hobby enjoyment, occasionally the remnants of "a social life." Help me not to feel the stress and pressure as one great whole, Lord, but to take each day as a separate challenge and to say no, without apology, to new requests for commitment of my time unless I really believe you are asking me to say yes. Help me to jealously guard some time each day for quiet, for Bible study, and for more-than-mealtime praying.

■ September 14

Lord, increase my desire for silence and my ability to establish it. Just silence. No TV, no radio, not even quiet Christian music. I seldom seek silence purposefully even when I have the opportunity, such as when I have the day off and the house to myself. And on a normal day, I might as well forget about it altogether. How often have I left the establishment of silence to a worship leader or a retreat director? Make me the scheduler of my own silence. Father, if you will show me the moments that are available for silence, I vow to be more faithful in choosing not to fill those moments with noise. Comfort me, sustain me, and speak to me in and through silence, I pray.

■ September 15

By your Spirit, the prophet Isaiah proclaimed that you will keep in perfect peace the one whose mind is stayed on you (Isa. 26:3). How enticing, the dream of perfect peace in this crazy and violent world. But I've found I'm unable in my own resources to keep my mind fixed on you, Lord. Help me! Make me confident of ultimate spiritual and physical victory when I turn my mind toward you. Give me peace! Like the fictional Superwoman, I want to soar. I need something higher and removed from all the noise, stuff, and junk. I will soar not by magical powers, but by your supreme and eternal power, Most High God.

■ September 16

Many times I have realized, loving Lord, that you go before me, with me, and behind me. You prepare me ahead of time, you give me the right words at the moment, and later you build on what was said and done. Thank you for loving and guiding me in these ways through critical marital discussions, moments of important parenting, and unexpected confrontations with school-teachers or store clerks. Help me begin every day verbalizing my need of you for whatever moments that day will bring. You'll be there, anyway, Lord, doing all sorts of things for me that I seldom realize. I believe you'll do even more if I ask you to.

■ September 17

Father, I'm annoyed with myself for getting so annoyed at my kids' noisemaking. I react, "Hey! Do you have to be so *loud?*" I used to be more enthralled by my children, Lord. I used to give them more undivided attention. Am I getting less patient, or just more selfish? Please keep me from making my children feel like an inconvenience. They live in a child's world; help me adjust to that and readjust as my needs and their needs change. As for their need to be noisy, help me embrace that with a little more love and patience, guiding them toward quieter behavior only when necessary.

■ September 18

Lord, your Word really *is* "a lamp to my feet and a light to my path" (Ps. 119:105) if I'll just read it. Thank you for this vivid word picture of a device shedding light on the path a few feet ahead rather than illuminating distant objects. I will try to narrow my focus to the next few steps, not worrying about *everything* that may lie beyond. Forgive me for keeping my Bible closed, like a flashlight carried in the dark but not switched on. I need rays of insight and comfort! In a moment of free time, cause me to be as likely to pick up my Bible as I am to pick up a library book or the TV remote.

September 19

Father, my long mental to-do list is going to get even longer when I write it down. Help me remain calm. Show me what must be done, what can wait, and what should be dismissed altogether. Keep me from characterizing this day only by how many tasks get done. I should not judge any day's meaning or success only by how long and detailed its completed agenda was. Give me joys and feelings that can't be listed on paper! I want moments invested in things I can't see or describe, discovered as I pour out my heart to you in prayer. Father, keep me here, *in this very spot,* until what needs to get done, here and now in prayer, is in fact done.

September 20

Confession time, Lord: badmouthing. Gossiping about people's shortcomings as I see them. Lord, this is wrong, even if the bad-mouthing is just in my mind. Help me to shut off inappropriate thoughts more quickly. Change me into the kind of person to whom such thoughts don't even occur! At church we're heard to say, "If gossip starts, the right thing to do is remove yourself from the group or say, 'Let's change the subject; we're not helping Mrs. What's-her-name by talking about her this way. Let's pray for her instead, and pray that we will become less judgmental and more accepting.'" Please guide me to act, not just talk, that way.

▰ September 21

Lord, help me lead my children, by example, away from trying to look "cool" by cutting another person down with smart and sarcastic remarks. This is not just a schoolyard fad. It goes on in the workplace. It goes on at church. It goes on in me. I see bad hair at the mall. I mention it to my companions whisperingly. Or I see a fashion disaster and laugh to myself or point it out to a friend or a daughter. Quick to ridicule; slow to learn. I need forgiveness and I need growth. I don't want to go on spouting derision. Other things—nice, true, helpful, serious things—are so much more beneficial to think about and talk about.

▰ September 22

Thank you, God, for the arrival of autumn! Thank you in advance for the mental and physical relief cooler weather will bring. Help me enjoy the autumn this year, Lord, even though life will be busy. Thank you for the warm feelings I associate with the cooler season, stemming from years of memories of back-to-school and Thanksgivings and Christmases, all of which are rolled up into one generalized, inexplicable, *excited* feeling that seizes me at unexpected moments when autumn comes around each year. Help me do what I can to foster a similar experience in my family and in others.

▰ September 23

Lord God, if my overall life is supposed to be an offering to you, that means the small portions of my conduct, in routine tasks and nonroutine situations, must be in service to you. I do not ask you to make me "worthy" to serve you, because I can never be that. I will just ask you to make me *able* to serve you in any way you require. This is my heartfelt desire. If some of my physical ability goes away over time and I can no longer perform certain physical tasks, then enable me to be productive and helpful to you and to other people in other ways.

▰ September 24

Thank you, dear Lord, for my family. I get annoyed with them at times; make me stop in my tracks more often to be amazed at who they are and what they do. Thank you for when they make me laugh and for the cute cards they give me on special occasions. Thank you for my children's special works of art, their bear hugs, and their *Hey, Mom! Guess what?*s. Thank you for the love each member of my family shows me every day by accepting responsibility and just "being family." I am thankful for all my family does that's good, helpful, and responsible; prompt me to express my appreciation to them.

▰ September 25

Teach me, Lord Jesus, not to be "worried and distracted by many things" as Martha was (Luke 10:41). You told her, "there is need of only one thing," and Mary chose that one thing (v. 42). Luke tells us Mary sat at your feet and listened to what you were saying. Is it possible, Lord, that a multitasking, Mary-Martha combination personality "super woman" in post-*everything* culture can still settle on that one thing that will put all the rest into perspective? It sounds so simple but seems so difficult. All things are possible for you, dear Lord. Help me simplify the "many things" and focus more on the "one thing"—you.

▰ September 26

I want to seek you with all my heart, God, being promised in your Word that if I do that, I will find you (Jer. 29:13). I desire this for others, too, not just for myself. I am bothered by the fact that this and other simple-sounding promises of Scripture can be so elusive and frustrating to us in our human struggle. If we are not understanding correctly what is promised in Scripture, send the wise counsel of your Spirit to make things clear. If we are listening to what others *say* the Bible says rather than reading it firsthand, bring us face-to-face with your Word and open our understanding as we read.

▰ September 27

The writer of Psalm 44 called out from a sense of being unjustly forsaken by you, God: "Our heart has not turned back, nor have our steps departed from your way, yet you have broken us . . . and covered us with deep darkness" (vv. 18–19). When we become convinced that we are following your ways and we do not understand why you have not granted certain prayer requests in response to our faithfulness, help us. If we are so sure of our guiltlessness, are we not then guilty of pride? "If we had forgotten the name of our God, or spread out our hands to a strange god, would not God discover this? For he knows the secrets of the heart" (Ps. 44:20–21). Search us out, God!

▰ September 28

Reach deep within me, Lord, to point out and remove my pride, my wrong assumptions about you, and all other sins I am committing even as I strive to obey you. I ask this not as a means of figuring out how to get you to give me particular things I desire. Let me learn to gauge your blessing in my life not by the number of possessions and joys you have given me but by how eager I have become to pursue an intimate relationship with you. Wonderful God, I long to understand blessing in a very different way from how I have thought of it most of my life! Bless me abundantly, I pray.

▬ September 29

My Lord Christ, you ask of me no more than you have given for me: all. I know that. I want to give you lordship in all of my life, difficult as it is for me to do. And I don't want to stop there. On a television program called *Jeopardy!*, contestants lose money when they ask the wrong questions. I don't want to lose spiritual wealth because I am asking the wrong question. Maybe "How much does Christ expect from me?" is the wrong question for me now. I suspect the right question is, "How much can I give to Christ?"

▬ September 30

Father, I crave for myself and for my children a generation unlike the one described in Psalm 78:8, which was stubborn and rebellious, whose heart was not steadfast, whose spirit was not faithful to you. Help me teach your commands, especially by example, to my children's generation, so that they may do the same in turn for their children. For this and for all things, great God, I need your enabling, your strength, and your power, since I'm not Superwoman! Above all, work on my heart. Grow within me the desire and the ability to live for you with energy and joy.

october

when shall we lie down in green pastures?

The LORD is my shepherd, I shall not want. He makes me lie down in green pastures; he leads me beside still waters; he restores my soul. He leads me in right paths for his name's sake.

PSALM 23:1–3

meditation on a psalm

Gone, it seems, the days we called "carefree."
Honest need.
When, O Lord, in want shall we not be?

Larger loom the tasks in this ravine.
Endless work.
When shall we lie down in pastures green?

Rocky seems the path we tread uphill.
Obstacles.
When shall we be led by waters still?

Toil, and fatigue seems our reward.
Weariness.
When, O Lord, will our souls be restored?

Scarcer are the things that make us laugh.
Fear and stress.
When shall we feel comfort from thy staff?

Love we sometimes crave, and then we know.
None to spare.
When will this cup start to overflow?

Lord, this world does oft exclude us well.
Alien.
When in thy house shall we ever dwell?

See again your precious Savior bleed,
And that is when you will not be in need.

Carefully your duties redefine,
And then in pastures green will you recline.

Daily with my words be filled and fed,
And then by quiet streams will you be led.

Learn to live a life of slower pace,
And then your soul will find a resting place.

Honestly commit to me each thing,
And then my guiding hand will comfort bring.

Never let the truth of my love dim,
And then will love surpass your vessel's rim.

Give, within, my Spirit greater roam,
And in my presence you will make your home.

▬ October 1

Psalm 23:2 reads: "He makes me lie down in green pastures." Father, do I have to be *made* to lie down? Probably so. You may be saying, "Stop," but all I want to do is go. With a gentle hand you may push me down for rest, but like a weighted punching bag I pop back up. I need to practice enjoying leisure. And it's not always someone else I have to fend off in order to have leisure—often, it's me. If I choose to relax and watch an old movie, invariably I feel I must be doing something else at the same time: hemming a skirt, sorting coupons, *something*. Lord, teach me to lie down and just rest!

▬ October 2

Still my heart, Lord. Quiet my restless mind. My doubts, questions, and speculations often are not useful or constructive. In your shepherdlike love and wisdom, reveal to me the positive side of things. Guard me from becoming more negative as I grow older. Help me overlook minor annoyances. Fill up my empty spaces! Even though my hours are crammed full of activity, there are spaces in my time and in my thoughts that I tend to fill with things of questionable value. Keep me on worthy, wholesome, and safe paths, Lord. I don't want to be running off here and there when I need to be following you.

▬ October 3

Lord and Shepherd, I thank you for your strong arms. Lord Jesus, your shepherding arms are the same arms that formed the planets, the stars, and every other intricate particle of matter. I thank you that your arms are strong enough to remove obstacles and ward off threats, but also gentle enough to rock me to sleep when I finally have the sense to write "resume here later" on my too long to-do list.

October 4

When I have allotted a couple of hours in the morning for a half-dozen errands before my "real" agenda of the day begins, Lord, I am tempted to rush into what I see as trivial tasks when the truth is that something big could happen to or around me in that two-hour period. I need to be prepared for that. When I am thinking mainly of what comes next instead of what comes *now*, stop me! Lead me to empty my hands of car keys, purse, and outgoing mail, bow my head, and ask you to watch over me *all day*. Forgive me for thinking your guidance is essential only for certain "more important" parts of a day.

October 5

A child we call a "follower" actively imitates his or her peers, forgetting the original agenda and going with what the stronger personality wants to do. We generally discourage this in our children, but it's exactly what we need to do in our walk with you, the Good Shepherd. How unnatural it is in our adulthood to proudly exclaim, "I'm a follower!" We want to be leaders. We're encouraged from elementary school days to grow up and be leaders. Enable me to be a follower when it comes to you, my Good Shepherd! Holy Spirit, remake my heart so I follow gladly—not mindlessly, without individual identity, but as one uniquely gifted and uniquely loved.

▄ October 6

Lead me, Lord, in right paths. I may think I have a clear purpose in life and work generally, and I may know what I have to do daily to care for my family and myself. But an overall, *general* sense of "right purpose" is no guarantee I'll choose right paths as I pursue that purpose. What if I go about a right thing the wrong way? I've done that before. What if I grow too time-conscious and impatient, losing my temper with my husband or child while doing a good deed like preparing food for a neighbor who's had surgery? A day has paths on many levels, Lord. Lead me in the right ones.

▄ October 7

I've heard sermons on Psalm 23 in which preachers point out that sheep are really stupid animals. Lord, that doesn't exactly reassure me, given that your Word repeatedly compares people to sheep. But I admit it—I do wander into unknown and unsafe places. I stare at what you have led me to and have said is good for me, but I refuse to move forward and partake. Forgive me, Lord, for when I behave stupidly and stubbornly, trusting my own judgment and the voices of other sheep instead of following you.

▄ October 8

It bothers me, dear God, when we church members have trouble forgiving one another. Either vocally or just with our airs and actions, we hold some people's mistakes "unforgivable." Yet we speak out of the other side of our mouths a message of your complete forgiveness. Teach us that we cannot convey the message of forgiveness in two different versions. Because you forgave Peter for denying you, he did not stay crippled by guilt, nor was he ostracized by the other disciples. He had a powerful ministry, led by your Spirit. Lead us, too, dear Shepherd, out of bondage to the past into a powerful present!

▰ October 9

Psalm 88:13 reads, "But I, O LORD, cry out to you; in the morning my prayer comes before you." I may have a weekday routine that includes prayer but think prayer "unnecessary" on a Sunday morning because I'll be going to church in a little while. Caution me, Lord, not to look for my spiritual nurture only in church. Teach me, Lord, to focus, to pray, and to worship—in church, of course, but also at home and at other places. Cause my church experience to be a wonderful bonus in my spiritual life on top of everything I experience of you everywhere else, all through the week.

▰ October 10

Lord God, thank you for Bible passages that reveal real human emotions and struggles: distress, anguish, fear of death, inability to believe in your attention to difficult circumstances. In spite of their troubles, the writers of Scripture also expressed firm faith. Whether the setting is a shepherd's lonely hillside or a twenty-first-century home in suburbia that serves as the nerve center for a busy, multidirectional life, human questions and needs are real and important! God, uphold us with your mighty arms when we are distressed and confused. Rescue us from the whirlpool of our confounding "why" questions. Draw us into your Word and speak to us through your Spirit until our faith is secure.

155

▄ October 11

Dear Lord, guide my curious instincts. If the way has not been paved by you, then steer me clear of that path. On the other hand, I do want to be available when you call me to something that requires venturing out in faith. When a mother calls a child in for dinner, she calls the child to come in to where she already is. It's not "go over there" but "come here, where I am waiting." Father, when you issue a call, help us remember that you do not send us where you have not prepared the way. Help us remember this when we hear your call to minister to a neighbor or to go abroad as a missionary.

▄ October 12

Thank you, loving Lord, for being a shepherd who goes out looking for the lost and the hurt, gathering each one, dirt and all, into your arms and returning it to the safety and comfort of the fold. An arrogant, uncaring shepherd might go out and purchase other sheep instead of seeking the lost ones, much as fly-by-night businesses treat their customers. Lord, it's clear that *you* experience loss when your followers get lost. Thank you for not being satisfied with a flock of 99 if you started out with 100.

▄ October 13

Lord Jesus, forgive me for when I listen primarily to other sheep and take my focus off your Word and your voice. We sheep have become quite expert at self-justification based on what everybody else is doing. If I'm not doing that, I may be chasing my own shadow, fluctuating between conviction and doubt. Sometimes I pray and I know that instead of a clear answer from you, all I'm able to hear at the moment is my own logic as I bounce options around. Lead me, Lord, beside still waters. Let me be silent long enough and often enough to hear you and to know I've heard you.

▰ October 14

Heavenly Father, I believe that in some sense our lives should hum along like well-maintained machinery if we are doing our work, keeping our homes and personal lives in order, trusting you for guidance, and accepting the spiritual peace you give. But something about the idea of just "clicking along" bothers me, if steady and comfortable routine means complacency and unwillingness to endure real inconvenience in order to help someone. Show me when to take a determined detour from my smooth road for the benefit of another person.

▰ October 15

Lord Jesus, I grow dependent on past experience, on familiarity, on tracks left by the sheep that went down the path yesterday. I mustn't forget about my Shepherd, for this reason among many others: my routine is going to be disrupted now and then by tragedy or by change that I am not comfortable with. At those crunch times may it be clear that my faith life is not separate from my "regular" life. Lord Jesus, I deeply desire to see my spiritual nature become inseparable from work, home life, hobby life, and all other "aspects" of my life. I desire to know your presence at all times and to follow your voice whether the path is familiar or strange.

▬ October 16

Lord God, if I thrive in overdrive, it is because you enable me to do that. Please give me the physical and mental energy my busy life requires. But when the time comes to slow down, by choice or by obligation, help me make the best of it. When I must put my own projects on hold to attend a wedding or to do what the rest of the family wants to do, help me appreciate the change of scenery and the people who are there. Teach me to function in low gear without being impatient. I want to lie down in green pastures instead of always choosing to speed by, noticing a green blur out of the corner of my eye and wondering what it is.

▬ October 17

Psalm 23:3 proclaims, "He leads me in right paths for his name's sake." Lord, if I call myself your child, yet wander into sin, it dishonors your name. If I speak of your great leadership but demonstrate poor followership, it presents a confusing message to others. You have revealed your name and your identity in mighty ways throughout history. You are still revealing yourself to people who are still asking, "Is there a God? Where is God? Does God care about me?" If my staying in right paths will help others know you, Lord, then in right paths is where I will strive to be.

▬ October 18

David, in Psalm 23, claimed, "Even though I walk through the darkest valley, I fear no evil; for you are with me" (v. 4). Lord, if I am walking *through* the valley, I eventually will reach the other side. Thank you for the tremendous meaning carried even in a single word of Scripture! Thank you for carrying me through my darkest valleys. Help me learn to say, like David, "I fear no evil." I'm not there yet! I wish I weren't so ready to believe that any given stranger is up to no good, but I never want to look back upon tragedy and say, "I should have been more cautious." Lord, help me function with appropriate caution but without unnecessary fear.

▬ October 19

Lord, you are with me. I am always ready to recall that fact when I am afraid; let me also remember it at work, when doing dishes, when laughing with friends, and when choosing a movie to rent. Let me feel comfort from your rod and staff not only because they defend me, but because they indicate your authority. Children need to know their boundaries to feel safe and confident, the experts say. I have a great desire to stay in the boundaries you have set for me, Lord. Let your rod and staff remind me that I don't rule. You do. You are God. I am not my own god or anyone else's. I'm not Superwoman. I am your child. Lead me, Lord.

▬ October 20

"The boundary lines have fallen for me in pleasant places; I have a goodly heritage," the psalmist professed (Ps. 16:6). Wait a minute. "Boundary" and "pleasant" in the same sentence? Father God, our human nature wants to understand pleasure as the absence of any restriction! But our understanding is not like yours. All-wise God, help us see that you provide boundaries for our good. Rules are necessary for any group to function most efficiently; we accept that pretty well. Give us the wisdom, Lord, to place ourselves in your fold knowing that within its boundaries are the most pleasant places we could hope to find.

October 21

Dear loving Shepherd, thank you for the wisdom you give, which sometimes comes through the testimony of others who have learned from both good and bad experiences. Make me less determined to figure certain things out for myself and more willing to learn from leaders you have called into positions of responsibility and authority. Often jealousy keeps me from being a good follower. Lead me in right paths regarding this while protecting me from falling victim to wolves in shepherds' clothing.

October 22

Precious Savior, with great love and great awe I extend my voice and my heart to you now. Lord Jesus, I need forgiveness for continuing to behave as if I am the most important person in the world. Sure, I serve my family and try to defer to others' preferences in this situation or that, but lurking under it all is a constant focus on *my* life, *my* needs, *my* hopes and dreams. Lord Christ, *you* are the most important person in the world. Build in me the ability to think and behave out of an unswerving desire to know you, to love you, and to make others more aware of who you are.

October 23

"You prepare a table before me in the presence of my enemies" (Ps. 23:5). Thank you, God, for this reminder that when opposition is present, it doesn't mean you are absent. It's tempting to think our troubles come because our Shepherd was gone or was just not paying attention, but Scripture does not teach that you neglect or ignore your people. When enemies see your provision, I pray that they will be intrigued rather than frustrated and more oppressive. I believe, Lord, that your intent is not to anger and taunt people who are outside your fold but to draw them in by showing that you provide.

October 24

So much debate goes on, dear Shepherd, about the respective roles of husband and wife. What does Scripture say about it, and what does Scripture mean? What is God's way, and what is culture's gradual influence? Remind me, Lord, that sometimes it is just as hard for my husband to submit to the Scripture that declares he is head of the household (Eph. 5:23) as it is for me to accept that as his role. Help us, Lord, to honor you by not squabbling about whose wishes will prevail. Only then will we have a peaceful household. Help me and my husband as we seek to follow you, wise Shepherd, and as we seek to love and serve one another.

October 25

References to people doing what is right and wise in their own eyes appear in Deuteronomy, Judges, Job, Psalms, Proverbs, and Isaiah. Apparently the problem was big enough in Bible times to need addressing repeatedly. I can see why, Father. We still tend to believe we are our own best guides. When we do not have a common standard of what is right, we have no consensus, no unity, and no lasting progress toward a better world to live in. If we propose to be shepherds to ourselves, we will wander and get lost. Open our eyes, Lord God! Guide us toward common goals that are based on your standards.

▬ October 26

Before Psalm 23 speaks of mental and spiritual blessing, it deals with physical needs—water, food, and protection from nature and enemies. Lord Jesus, you healed physical ailments as you taught about the kingdom of God. You fed hungry crowds, saved the disciples from a violent storm, and even dealt with a social crisis by turning water into the wine expected by the wedding guests at Cana. Jesus, you lived in the "real world" as seen by the people back then, even though your message was that the *actual* real world was something entirely different! Help us, Lord Jesus, to follow your example in our day.

▬ October 27

Forgive me, Lord, for continuing to arrange the time at my disposal so that too many days are filled and prayer time gets edged out. Neglecting to spend time in prayer with my Shepherd amounts to neglecting *myself.* It is neglecting my best interests, for you have my best interests at heart always. John 10:9 reads, "I am the gate. Whoever enters by me will be saved, and will come in and go out and find pasture." Amazing. The Christian life restrictive? I don't think so. Not when the Shepherd promises salvation, mobility, and provision. Wow! Your love is incredible. That's why I want to know you and love you more.

▬ October 28

Lord, we crave independence. We don't want to be weak or to lose our identity. We don't want to feel that we are part of a huge flock of dumb sheep being led along. We want notoriety. Distinction. Something great accomplished that we will be remembered for. Teach us, God, that greatness is found in great dependence on you. Lead us to find our unique value and establish our unique contribution to the universe inside your protective and pleasant sheepfold. Scripture declares repeatedly that you create humans with individual gifts and with individual value. Thank you for loving us individually and speaking to our specific needs every day.

October 29

Thank you, Lord, for the beautiful color and life the dying leaves bring to my surroundings and my attitude. Add in the blessed relief from summer heat, and autumn remains something to celebrate! Add in the anticipation of the holidays, and it's no wonder many people call this time of year their favorite. Thank you for ministering to us seasonally in your wisdom, Lord. "Special times" wouldn't be special if they were with us every day. Help us enjoy the times we love best, and help us find greater stamina, and even joy, in the times we would call humdrum.

October 30

I haven't the words to thank you, God, for the security I feel because of these words: "I give [my sheep] eternal life, and they will never perish. No one will snatch them out of my hand" (John 10:28). I have security *now*, but someday I will cross over into your full presence, God. I will be united forever with the Source of my existence. I will feel I am coming home, at long last, to where I've always wanted to be. For that to happen, I must not keep you distant now. Seek after me, God, as I seek after you! Show yourself to me. Make your ways known to me. I can't wait to know you much more than I know you now!

163

▬ October 31

O Lord, I desperately need the wisdom and the humility to allow myself to be shepherded by you (and to understand that doing so does not take anything away from me, but adds so much to me!). I never want to hear you say to me as you said to the city of Jerusalem, "See, your house is left to you" (Luke 13:35). Woe words, indeed. Lord Jesus, please do not leave my house to me! I am not the one to lead it. You are welcome here. You are wanted here, in my house—literally in every room and on every inch of the property. And you are wanted in the house that is *me:* my thoughts, my body, my soul.

november

two steps forward

Do not, therefore, abandon that confidence of yours; it brings a great reward.

HEBREWS 10:35

senior moments

They've come to be known as "senior moments."
The goofy, forgetful, airheaded things I do more often now than
    before, like
      leaving the soft drink cup on top of my car and driving away;
Looking all over for the pair of earrings I intended to put on,
    finally discovering I'd already put them on;
Having to tape notes to the mirror, to the door,
    and to the middle of my car's steering wheel more and more
      often,
      just to be able to remember all the little "this and thats" I'm
        supposed to do;
Forgetting phone numbers, mental grocery lists, and where I
    parked the car;
Plunging my hand into the dishwater wearing a potholder glove
    instead of the yellow rubber glove I'd intended to put on;
Using vocabulary I once considered hokey and out of touch, like
    "lovely";
Forgetting what I needed from the pantry in the time it took to
    walk over there;
Interrupting a conversation, sometimes,
    to express a thought for fear I'll forget it if I don't say it *now;*

Admitting (and accepting) that I'll never again attempt
    a cartwheel
  unless there's an urgent need for a person with a broken wrist.

But there are good senior moments, too,
  like achieving a long-awaited and years-worked-for goal.
And moments that happen because, as a more senior adult than I
    used to be,
  I've learned some important things and learned how to use what
    I've learned.

Thank you, Lord, for the good senior moments.

Thank you for the times I haven't voiced the careless or unkind
    remark that came to mind,
  because in a senior moment of wisdom
  I've realized that voicing it would only do harm.

Thank you for the times I've stayed silent altogether,
  because in a senior moment of reticence
  I've realized that while my opinions are still important,
  it is not always important to state them, especially when
    it seems
  there is already plenty of noise in the world.

Thank you, Lord, for the times I have not stayed silent,
  because in a senior moment of confidence and boldness
  I've realized that something I learned earlier in life applied
  to a younger person's situation and might be helpful if shared.

Thank you for the times I've refused to allow frustration
  with certain external situations to get me down,
  because in a senior moment of patience

I've realized that right-now frustrations often are baseless
and that many back-when frustrations
have sorted themselves out over time.

Thank you for the times I've chosen
    not to wallow in irrational fear of the future,
    because in a senior moment of confidence in your Word
    I've been comforted by your promise of unfailing love
    and eternal security for my immortal soul.

Bless me, O Lord, in every senior moment, good or bad.
Thank you, Lord, for sending new kinds of blessings
    to replace others that are changing or gradually disappearing.
Watch over me, Lord, as I grow older.

And let me truly *grow* older, not just get older.

▆ November 1

Please forgive me, Lord, for the times I have giggled or felt superior when an older person was walking very slowly, having trouble hearing, or just looking really, really aged. In the immaturity of my youth, that was a natural reaction sometimes. But I'm a lot closer to that situation now. I ask forgiveness because it was and is wrong to laugh at another's infirmity or personal difficulty. I do want to laugh kindly with my friends who are experiencing the silly "senior moments" along with me, though. Our talk has gradually shifted from how many batters we struck out last week to how many doctors we saw last month. Senior moments. But may I live long enough to have a lot of them!

▆ November 2

Lord God, knowing how important it is that young people receive sufficient personal affirmation and positive feedback as they learn new skills, help me do all I can to encourage them. Younger people used to depend on my ability and knowledge a lot. Soon that will be all turned around. The older I get, the more dependent I will be on younger people. They will be the teachers of my children and grandchildren, the doctors I rely on, and the officials I help elect. Lord, make me a lifelong learner so that even when I am very old, I will still have something to contribute. And if I know something I should share, let me share it humbly, not in a way that will annoy others.

▆ November 3

Dear Lord, I'm getting to the point where everything "retro" seems best. I like the look of dishes, books, and lunch boxes that were around when I was a kid. Instead of current television programs, I prefer to watch the shows I grew up on. You must have wired people to enjoy nostalgia. Help me enjoy looking back, but also open my eyes to new things that might add value to my life if I would give them a chance. After all, some of my current favorite candy bars didn't even exist when I was ten years old! Lord, when I miss being in the high school band or being able to turn a cartwheel, remind me that there is still plenty left for me to do and do well.

▬ November 4

Father in heaven, I look in the mirror and I don't like what I see. Gray hair. Laugh lines. *Jowls,* for crying out loud! (I thought those things belonged on animals, not people.) Please help me when I am distressed by the unattractive things aging is doing to my body; I can't really change much of that—not for long, anyway. And there is something *good* about growing older: the acquisition of wisdom. Source of all wisdom, continue to transform me into the likeness of Christ my Lord. Remind me that appearance is temporary as I invest passionately in what is permanent.

▬ November 5

Lord Jesus, may I embrace the aging process by focusing less on my body's deterioration and more on what I am gaining, like valuable learning. Thank you for the lessons only time can teach, like finding joy in turning the spotlight on other people to build them up rather than constantly trying to be the center of attention myself. We all need praise and affirmation; maybe we try to fish for it now because we didn't receive enough of it at the age we needed it most. But Proverbs 27:2 instructs, "Let another praise you, and not your own mouth." Father, I am not only the "you" in that verse; I am also the "another" who needs to affirm the people around her.

▰ November 6

Thank you, God, for leading me sometimes to pray using the public telephone directory as my guide. It feels a bit strange calling aloud names of people I've never met, but I believe you hear and are working miracles because I pray for those people by name. You know their needs; I am merely a willing vessel in the working of your plan. This is powerful! I trust what your Word teaches about prayer, and I am going to act on it as much as I can, in as many ways as I can.

▰ November 7

Holy God, keep me aware always that your ways are not the ways of the human intellect or will. What seems like a logical, reasonable assessment of a situation may not be at all what I would see if I were looking with eyes guided by you! Help me know that in spite of all the fact-finding I can do, I may have missed an angle. As I try to be wise and mature, remind me that my ability comes from you and from no other source. Culture hails the empowerment of the individual; fine, as long as it is you empowering me because I have chosen to be submissive to you.

▰ November 8

Dear Lord, teach us to be students of the Bible so we will not try to apply its words out of context, "proving" that it teaches something we want to believe it teaches. Matthew 19:26 says "but for God all things are possible." Father, just because something is possible for you doesn't mean it is your plan for that something to occur. Possible, yes. Promised, no. Guaranteed to happen if I have "enough" faith, no! Even though all things are possible for you, that does not mean I can expect that what I wish would happen will happen. Help me love and revere you, Lord, because of who you are, not because of what I'd like you to do for me.

▬ November 9

Dear Lord, children seldom love naptime. Stop playing to lie down and rest? Inconceivable! Why would a parent demand that? Now I have learned that naps are a rare and cherished luxury! Sleep, no matter the time of day or night, is like the darkness, silence, and warmth that characterized being in the womb. It is a refuge. You created us to need rest. Just as we need discipline to eat neither too much nor too little, give us the discipline to sleep in healthy amounts. When we're so driven to do and to succeed that we think, *Life is too short to waste it sleeping,* teach us that life is too short for us to refuse to be wise.

▬ November 10

Dear God, we are an "express" people. Express mail. Drive-through pharmacies. Microwave popcorn. We try to have express faith and spirituality, too, thinking we can satisfy our deep need of you with an hour of church on Sunday and snippets of feel-good Scripture now and then during the week. Give us a craving for more than snippets! Make us interested enough in truth and accuracy to be sure our favorite Bible verses really say what we think they say. And awaken in us the desire to learn what comes before and after our favorite Bible verses.

▰ November 11

Lord, as I remember my country's veterans, I ask that you will make me more aware, *every* day, that their diligent service, including making the ultimate sacrifice of life, has made possible the freedoms, comforts, and privileges I enjoy as an American. For so many to have set aside personal plans and dreams to serve and defend this nation is a sacrifice I don't comprehend and appreciate adequately, Lord. And that reminds me of another life—your life—whose sacrifice made an entirely different kind of freedom possible. Lord, for that and for the great nation I call my own, I am thankful! My words are insufficient, but my heart is grateful.

▰ November 12

Dear Lord, your name is "a strong tower" (Prov. 18:10). Make me less fearful of the world around me because this is true. If ever I needed a strong tower to run into for safety, it is now. I want to be comfortable calling your strong name aloud, without hesitation and without caring what anyone will think. Lord, many of us seek shelter inside towers we believe to be strong: a home where we feel loved, an education, a stable job, personal drive and energy, faithful friends, a strong country. Then we discover that those towers are precarious and frail; even if they are firmly rooted in faith, they still are imperfect. But your name is a strong tower that is perfect and unfailing.

▰ November 13

Lord God, give me the confidence that came to Hezekiah when he prayed before you, "O LORD the God of Israel, who are enthroned above the cherubim, you are God, you alone, of all the kingdoms of the earth; you have made heaven and earth. Incline your ear, O LORD, and hear; open your eyes, O LORD, and see" (2 Kings 19:15–16). In our land, in our day, your name and images that are supposed to represent you are tossed around in disgraceful ways in the name of art, in the name of free speech, and in the name of evil. How your people need confidence to respond to that, O God! Fill us with spiritual knowledge and power so we can proclaim who you are.

▰ November 14

Father God, amazing things happen when I read your Word with a seeking heart! Luke 14:1 begins an account of the Pharisees "watching Jesus closely" to see if they could trip him up and find him doing something of which they could accuse him. *Watching Jesus closely!* I must confess to you I do not watch Jesus as closely as I can watch him through the written accounts of his life. If I will spend more time watching Jesus' life closely and less time watching, critiquing, and imitating my friends, neighbors, and even fictional characters, I will find myself changing for the better.

▰ November 15

Father, make me more mature spiritually by enabling me to handle the little annoyances of this physical life with wisdom and with greater detachment. Lord, I find myself praying constantly that the people who bug me will change. Help *me* change. You are showing me that I need to pray more often for change in myself, knowing that if I do change for the better, my influence on others may change *them*.

▬ November 16

Convict my heart and my conscience, dear Lord, when I open my mouth to criticize what someone else is doing. Change me so that my impulse is not to gossip, but to pray—first, for my attitude to be loving rather than critical; second, for the other person's need, whatever it may be. If I notice that people's actions are wrong or immature, my first responsibility is to come to you in prayer, asking you to intervene for their benefit and for the benefit of whomever they may be hurting.

▬ November 17

O God, empower me to confront trouble when necessary rather than always trying to deny trouble's presence and to avoid its fallout. I don't intend to go looking for trouble; I don't intend to make a list of all the people I've ever thought of "giving a piece of my mind" and to proceed systematically to tell them off (although the idea sounds tempting)! Rather, give me the confidence and assertiveness to face a person bravely and say things that need to be said rather than having my soul and my stomach churn silently in that person's presence. Guide me, I pray, in what I say to whom and when.

▬ November 18

Father, I confess it's much easier to look the other way than to speak the truth in love to a person who needs to hear it. I fear I will violate one scriptural mandate, "first take the log out of your own eye" (Matt. 7:5), in order to fulfill another. I fear I will cause more harm than good, sparking defensiveness and anger rather than leading someone to turn from wrong. To say

"I see that you are being deceived" takes more faith and prior prayer even than witnessing to someone on an airplane. It takes extreme sensitivity to the Spirit. Lord, prepare me now to speak the truth in love when you call me to do that.

▬ November 19

Lord, there will be much talk of thankfulness in the next several days. How will this go over with persons who are hurting, angry, or bitter? Please help them through this season when they may not feel the thankfulness everyone else is talking about. Minister to those whose hurt is keeping them out of church and away from their Bibles. Every church experience is not helpful, Lord, and well-meaning people sometimes say the most dreadful things! But being in your house puts a person in a position to hear or see a helpful thing when it does happen. Please prompt the hurting to act on this so their hurt will have a fighting chance to find help.

▬ November 20

Thank you, Lord, for the expectation that during the Thanksgiving weekend there will be opportunity for some badly needed rest. Help me accomplish what I need to do between now and then, and please let me not be so rushed and selfish that I brush my family aside now in order to "serve" them later! I sometimes don't want to stop what I'm doing to play a game or read a book with my children. Remind me of how fast these years will go by, never to return. When big events have all of us on edge, help us to be more of a team and less in each other's way. Guide us to use with one another the basic manners we display toward friends and strangers.

■ November 21

Lord, we are disappointed, naturally, when our child gets cheated out of her big moment on stage because a mike wasn't turned on. We hurt for her and for ourselves. But give us the grace to be understanding. People aren't perfect. Mistakes happen. Keep us from letting a hothead burst of fuming, either inward or outward, ruin the example we set for our children under circumstances like that. Give us the grace to pray for a person whose mistake, small or large, has hurt us or someone we love. Move us to extend the same generosity of attitude we will want from others when the situation is reversed.

■ November 22

When I call you "Father," I think of the parental love, protection, and correction you give for my well-being. When I address you as "Jesus," I envision the man of compassion and friendship who endured temptation, ridicule, suffering, and death. And when my thoughts need guidance and my spiritual vision needs clarity, I call on you, Holy Spirit. You minister to those needs and you also intercede for me—and those I pray for—with sighs my words cannot convey (Rom. 8:26). Holy God, make me more knowledgeable of your three-sided persona. And however I address you, may I always do so with reverence and with a willingness to hear your answer.

■ November 23

God, make me more aware every day of your supremacy and superiority. I believe that focusing on these realities will change the way I pray, and my prayers need to change, reflecting more confidence and victory! I am convinced there is great victory in reach when I am bold enough to *proclaim* the victory that does, in fact, belong to you and your people. I am convinced that feeling defeated is the same as being defeated. I don't want to wait until I get to heaven to feel I've experienced victory. Give me your power as I delve into your Word seeking truth and victory in this complex life. Complex life demands a woman who is effective because of your power.

▰ November 24

Lord, I've been feeling surges of thankfulness since the arrival of autumn. I am always amazed this time of year at the rich blue sky, the trees' brilliant color, and the fallen and falling leaves in so many sizes, shapes, and degrees of crunchiness under my feet! Remind me that heaven will be unimaginably more breathtaking than the most gorgeous autumn day, even though I don't understand how that could be possible. Lord, I thank you for my home and family, for work and rest and health, for special friends and much, much more. Most of all, I thank you for the assurance that nothing can ever separate me from your love.

▰ November 25

Dear Lord, writers of hymns and of Scripture have boldly claimed that human struggles are a gift from you and that we should rejoice when we have trials (James 1:2). But let's be honest. When personal problems rage, to be told that trials are a source of joy can make us skeptical at best, bitterly cynical at worst. I've seen that reaction in my friends and in myself. What can we do when words that are meant to comfort us actually make us feel worse? At those times I will continue to beg you for comfort, for what else can I do? Who else can help? Keep me faithful to you, Lord, and able to believe the Bible even—no, *especially*—when it's difficult.

■ November 26

Father, as the signs of preparation for Christmas appear, prepare me to "walk in the light of the LORD" (Isa. 2:5). Let the construction your Spirit is doing inside me be visible both to me and to others. Work in me to the point that I honestly find more joy in self-sacrifice than in self-gratification. Make me quicker to set my work or hobby aside and give time and attention to others, even if they haven't specifically asked me to do that. I know I will be glad in the short run and in the long run if I use my time less selfishly. I know I will find in that a mature type of joy that will be a great reward.

■ November 27

Dear Lord, as I look around my house and think about cleaning it in preparation for holiday decorating and drop-in guests, I also think about the cleanliness I need in my heart. "You desire truth in the inward being; therefore teach me wisdom in my secret heart. . . . Create in me a clean heart, O God, and put a new and right spirit within me" (Ps. 51:6, 10). I want to be made clean voluntarily, not by your having to drag me kicking and screaming to be dunked in the river. I desire to conform to your will and to obey your Word. Forgive my sins, precious Jesus; renew my purity before the Father through the blood poured out for me.

▬ November 28

Lord Jesus, Luke chapter 12 records a parable you spoke about a rich man who planned to build bigger barns to store the wealth he had accumulated self-centeredly, not knowing that his hours were numbered. God asked him, "The things you have prepared, whose will they be?" (v. 20). My hours are numbered, too, Lord. Whatever I call "mine" will be someone else's, eventually, unless it is treasure I have accumulated in my soul. Show me, Lord, how to live so that I am preparing things worthy of being left to others—tangible things like heirloom objects and intangible things like love and good influence.

▬ November 29

Thank you, loving Lord, for another lesson learned over the long years: that what I do and how important it seems is different from my value as a person. If I let how much I can or can't do determine how I feel about myself, what will happen to my self-image when my health begins to limit my activity? I want to do important things for as long as I can; I believe you want that, too. But don't let me confuse ability with personal worth. The fact that you love me and have given me intrinsic value is established. This is the fact that remains when everything else becomes a nonissue.

▬ November 30

Lord God, I am dependent on your goodness. It is what makes me want to love you and serve you. But even when I wander in confusion or defiance, your goodness keeps you faithful to me. When I realize the futility and danger of straying outside your fold, I come running back to your goodness. And you run out to meet me, as the father ran to welcome his lost son who was returning (Luke 15:20). Father, I want a closer bond of love between us. Keep me secure and comfortable with you. Guide me, I pray, to take two steps forward. And I will not look back, except to see how far you have brought me.

december

when i was a child . . .

Truly I tell you, whoever does not receive the kingdom of God as a little child will never enter it.

MARK 10:15

when I was a child

When I was a child,
    I walked to the store to spend my nickels on candy.
    I rode my bicycle alone, sometimes for miles.
    I licked the beaters and rolled in the grass.
    I loved my dog, hated working in the garden,
        and was afraid of lightning and thunder.
    I was not afraid of nuclear and biological warfare.

When I was a child,
    Christmas was a time of wide-eyed wonder
        with houses trimmed in lights
        and streets lined with decorations.
    I feasted at big family dinners with good china
        and bad congealed salad.
    I ate pulled mint candy that only Grandma made.
    I thrilled upon finding my name among the tags
        on the shiny red and green packages under the tree.
    I got a feeling of tremendous excitement and wealth
        when a money card from a favorite uncle
        revealed Lincoln's face through the oval cutout.
    I knew the pleasure of being entrusted with a few lines
        in the church Christmas pageant

and memorizing most of the other speaking parts, too,
    during umpteen rehearsals.
When I was a child,
    the ultimate task was to become an adult.
  Now that I am an adult,
    I need to rediscover how to be childlike.
Father in heaven, remind me that many aspects of childhood
    are assets throughout life. Renew my ability
        to be easily amused,
        to play without watching the clock,
        to believe things that are beyond my understanding,
        to be utterly amazed.
Help me, dear Lord, to fill my adult life with more of the
    fascination, fun, fantasy,
        feelings, friendliness,
           freedom,
    and the faith I had . . .

When I was a child.

▰ December 1

Abba, Father, your Word says we must receive your kingdom as little children. As we prepare to celebrate the birth of Jesus, who is the gate to the kingdom (John 10:7), give us childlike anticipation and excitement. Where is childlike joy among the stresses of last-minute gift buying and wondering how we'll pay the Christmas bills? It must be there somewhere. Please help me find that joy and, along with it, a worshipful appreciation for the love gift that you gave to me by sending Jesus as the Christmas Child who reigned even as an infant lying in a manger.

▰ December 2

Almighty God, as I have come to perceive myself as more sophisticated than the me of a decade (or two) ago, I have become more complacent about things that used to amaze me. I would like to rediscover that feeling of great awe over how big you are! Forbid it, Lord, that I should fail to think *Wow!* when I try to comprehend you. Thank you for being big enough to be everywhere at once. Thank you for being big enough to care about every person in the world. Help me to respect your greatness in the way I use your name in my conversation.

▰ December 3

Teach me, dear Father, to trust you as a child trusts—with complete confidence and security. I have supports that I lean on in practical ways, but they are temporary provisions from you, and they may not always be there. Teach me to rely on, and to love, the giver, not the gift. Scripture warns against taking the trust that should be placed in you and placing it in walls (Deut. 28:52), riches (Ps. 52:7), beauty (Prov. 31:30), our own insight (Prov. 3:5), and *ourselves* (2 Cor. 1:9). Teach me, Lord, even as I strive to do great things as an empowered woman, to trust you with everything I do, everything I want, and everything I am.

■ December 4

Young children ask questions without fear of embarrassment. Then things change. God, grant me a lesser measure of inhibition, especially in my praying. I need to voice my doubts and questions so you can address them in a way I will understand. I need to claim spiritual victory with emphatic statements based on Scripture. I will physically walk the borders of my home address and declare it off-limits to Satan's work, regardless of what someone else might think. Help me, Lord, not to be embarrassed about exhibiting and exploring my faith in the presence of others—including you.

■ December 5

"Seeing is believing." This philosophy evolves somewhere between the blind belief of childhood and I-won't-be-fooled adulthood. But, Lord Jesus, you said to Thomas, "Blessed are those who have not seen and yet have come to believe" (John 20:29). The apostle Paul wrote, "We walk by faith, not by sight" (2 Cor. 5:7). And Proverbs 25:7–8 warns, "What your eyes have seen do not hastily bring into court." Obviously we can't rely heavily on what we see—or think we see. Give us faith to believe without seeing. Give us restraint from reporting what we have seen (gossiping), and give us discernment of a friend's difficulty when appearance says, "Everything's fine."

▰ December 6

As the father of a sick child said, "Help my unbelief!" (Mark 9:24). Father, help me *believe* that the energy I invest in knowing you will result in more blessing than any self-focused pursuit of happiness could ever bring. Acting on this belief is faith—faith not for "miracles" in the usual sense but for the great miracle it takes inside to move me to choose that better thing. Faith is choosing to spend time searching for spiritual treasure as I would search for gold in my backyard if I believed gold was there. Lord, I believe. Turn my belief into the actions of a maturing spiritual woman.

▰ December 7

One of the wise sayings heard since childhood is "Listen more than you talk"—a paraphrase of any number of Bible verses about taming the tongue. Father, when I neglect to pray for your Spirit's control over what I say, I make insensitive statements, break confidences, and mouth off when I should be the one strong enough to be silent. Father, may the words of my mouth *and* the meditation of my heart be acceptable to you today (Ps. 19:14); if they are acceptable to you, they will not hurt the persons of whom and to whom I speak.

▰ December 8

"Like vinegar on a wound is one who sings songs to a heavy heart" (Prov. 25:20). Certain songs "of the season" are melancholy, Lord, indicating that everyone's experience of Christmas is not joyous. Grief, separation, and other struggles seem even worse when everyone else is talking about happy family times and calling, "Merry Christmas!" Make me sensitive to that, Lord, and make me responsive. At the same time, send your ministering angels to those whose pain and loss give them an acute need to know that the love you lavished upon the world in Jesus Christ includes them, too.

▰ December 9

Father, show me what attitude to take about the cultural traditions of Christmas. I tend to think that giving to my own family is not really giving but *getting,* since the gifts stay in my home and benefit everyone there. But I want to give gladly to my family and take pleasure in seeing their joy. Help me to remember and to remind my family and others that our festivity is about celebrating Jesus, our Savior. Teach me to anticipate and observe Christmas as a holy season above all else, Father. When that inexplicable "Christmas feeling" is in the air, let your Spirit say, *"What you are feeling is coming from me!"*

▰ December 10

More good advice learned in childhood: "Make new friends, but keep the old; one is silver and the other is gold." If I reserve my most vivacious self for a preferred inner circle, I may be passing up the opportunity to develop new and cherished friendships. Particularly in your house, Father, which is the least appropriate of all places to form and guard social cliques, make me willing to meet new people and become genuinely interested in knowing them. Growing in my social inclusiveness is a sign of spiritual maturity, Father. Teach me to grow in this area.

▰ December 11

As little children, we tended to talk freely. "How old are you?" "My grandpa died last year." "I'm going to be an astronaut." We trusted that people were interested in what we had to say, and it never occurred to us that an evil person might exploit our trusting nature. Then came growing up. It's difficult now, Lord, to reveal myself. It happens less frequently and with fewer people. Let me cultivate and cherish the relationships in which I can venture into that scary place called vulnerability. Time is a factor. Help me get unbusy enough to stop and talk to my husband and to my close friends, because when the talking diminishes, so does the closeness.

■ December 12

Keeping secrets and telling the truth—two large tasks we must learn as children and keep right on learning throughout life. Knowing something confidential is *power!* Thus we are tempted to use that to someone's disadvantage or to make ourselves look smart. "Do not disclose another's secret," says Proverbs 25:9. Lord, empower us to treat others' reputations as carefully as we treat our own. "You shall not bear false witness," directs Exodus 20:16. God, give us the moral strength to live without needing to hide with a lie anything we have done. Show us when to speak the truth and when to refrain from speaking at all.

■ December 13

Conventional wisdom says it this way: "Don't count your chickens before they're hatched." Proverbs 25:14 says it this way: "Like clouds and wind without rain is one who boasts of a gift never given." Bragging. It's no less a temptation now than it ever was, Lord God. Give me the sense not to proclaim something as a fact before the facts are in. Teach me not to disappoint my children by declaring we will take a trip to the movie store or the ice cream shop "today," later realizing that today is not the most convenient day for that. Words are so powerful, God. Let mine be chosen very carefully.

▬ December 14

O Lord, I listen to the radio and hear news about war and other tragedies while strains of "Joy to the World" sound in the background. What a juxtaposition! But this shows me how badly good news is needed. It was a troubled world when an angel proclaimed the true Good News of Jesus' birth. Thank you for seeing people's troubles then and sending Jesus. Thank you for seeing our troubles now and circulating the same Good News of salvation through Jesus.

▬ December 15

I thank you, Father, for crisp weather as a backdrop against which to ponder the warmth of new-parent joy that Mary and Joseph felt as they gazed at Jesus in his manger bed. Thank you for the holy glow that surely shone in the baby's face, and thank you for the warm feeling of joy that comes with celebrating his birth. Yet Christmas is not about how I feel but about what you did! No matter what is going on in my life right now, let me choose to honor Jesus' birth by celebrating it with happy festivity and with solemn worship.

▬ December 16

Taking turns. Sharing. Lessons begun while we are in diapers! Lessons that take a lifetime to learn. Here's another: moderation. Father, your Word is an endless trove of practical wisdom, addressing even this! "If you have found honey, eat only enough for you, or else, having too much, you will vomit it" (Prov. 25:16). Unpleasant picture, but it makes its point. Forgive me, Father, for when I've not shown moderation in my eating. Forgive me for accumulating more than I need because I could not withstand the temptation to go shopping. Teach me to find joy in acquiring moderately and sharing readily.

▬ December 17

When I was a child, my parents told me to set a good example. Lord Jesus, it would seem that you got the same instruction. You, in the very perfection of God the Father, could say without qualm, "I have set you an example, that you also should do as I have done to you" (John 13:15). Oh, that I could say the same to my children and really live up to my words. I need to be a good example for them. But, Jesus, I also need for them to know I am not perfect. I need for them to know that you are the one that they—and I—should be imitating.

▬ December 18

People once said that children should be seen but not heard. Lord, I desire to be the humble child who is the greatest in the kingdom of heaven (Matt. 18:4), seen by others as one who has been spending time with you. I desire not to be heard speaking the foolishness of my random and culture-coated thoughts but to be a conductor of *your* voice. When I walk into the grocery store, please let my appearance and my speech indicate that I am your child. I can't make that happen, Lord God. Only your Spirit can make that happen. By your Spirit, bless others through my life. Be seen and heard in me!

▰ December 19

Father, I need to be mature enough to admit my immaturity and get help! The young king Solomon and the young prophet Jeremiah each recognized his own inadequacy for the job. Solomon admitted, "I am only a little child; I do not know how to go out or come in" (1 Kings 3:7). And Paul advised Timothy, "Let no one despise your youth, but set the believers an example" (1 Tim. 4:12). I tend to assume I am wiser than younger persons and less crotchety than older persons. Give me more humility than that. Teach me to learn from and to set a good example for people of any age.

▰ December 20

Forgive me, Lord, when in need and frustration I am unwilling to see that your refusal of something is similar to a parent saying no to a childish request for more candy, a later curfew, or something else that's unwise. I explain to my children that a refusal is "for your own good" but fail to see that my wise heavenly parent does the same thing with me. Looking through eyes of childish want and oversimplification, I may think a certain situation or outcome seems right, but I must learn that there may be pitfalls that only you can see. I am going to wait for the situations you are preparing for me, the ones that you can eagerly say yes to.

▰ December 21

Lord, parents will be the first to say that obedience is not obedience unless it is immediate. I easily say that to a child and expect the child to measure up. But obedience to you seems more complicated than going to clean my room when a parent has told me to do that. Please reduce the noise of the culture and of my own self-centeredness as I turn my spiritual ears toward you. I want to hear and understand your wishes, Lord, so I can obey immediately. I want the childlike satisfaction of knowing you are pleased with how I have responded to your instructions.

December 22

Isaiah wrote, "Surely God is my salvation; I will trust, and will not be afraid" (Isa. 12:2). God, I know you are there. And here. Before me, behind me, and in my heart. As a child assumes that the parent who tucked her into bed at night will be there on call all night and will be there in the morning, I trust in your presence. I count on your parentlike protection. You are more dependable than the most dedicated and effective human parent. A human parent is, by definition, imperfect. But you are perfect. Help me know and accept your perfect will so I can avoid the dangers you desire for me to avoid and experience the joys you long to see me have.

December 23

Lord Jesus, your name is Emmanuel, "God with us." Psalm 23:4 declares, "I fear no evil; for you are with me." Precious Jesus, when every day brings reports of crime, terrorism, abuse, accidents, natural disasters, and unemployment, make me able to fear no evil *because you are God with me.* First John 4:4 reminds me that the one who is in me is greater than the one who is in the world. I will claim that in victory when fear disrupts my peace. And when the evidence of evil causes someone else to ask, "Where is God? Is God with us?", reveal yourself as God Almighty to that person.

▰ December 24

Lord Jesus, Prince of Peace, visit our home today! We invite you. We honor you. We have sought to prepare room for you. Fill our hearts as we go to bed anticipating the joy of Christmas morning. Give us peace in our strife- and sorrow-torn world. Lord, we did not see the dazzling display in the night sky when the heavenly host cried, "Glory to God in the highest!" But we anticipate seeing the glory of your return. Thank you that our greatest anticipation is not for the annual celebration of a past event (wonderful as that event was) but for a future event of unutterable beauty and glory.

▰ December 25

Heavenly Father, you sent light in the form of an angel's presence to signal the shepherds that the Messiah had been born. You sent light in the form of a brilliant star, a beacon, to guide the wise men to the stable where Jesus was. Lord, in every corner of the world, people are looking for the light. We need answers, direction, confidence, and love. Turn our eyes to the star of Bethlehem and from the star to the holy Child who is the Savior of the world. Oh, how we need Jesus, on every "normal" day and on every unusual day. Thank you for his blessed birth into our needy world!

▰ December 26

John chapter 9 records your healing of a man who had been blind since his birth. Lord Jesus, you could have restored his sight with a single word or just a thought. But you asked him to act in order for the healing to occur. He obeyed, washing in the pool of Siloam, and he was healed. You ask each person to respond, too, to the offer of spiritual healing. You offer the gift;

I can leave it under the tree, unopened, or I can reach out and take it. If I've already received the gift of you, help me keep the gift out, on display, and in use—all year long, unlike a Christmas toy that is soon forgotten.

▰ December 27

Jesus, you were born. How shall I respond? You are "the true light, which enlightens everyone" (John 1:9). Enlighten me! Not *generally*, but in specific thought cycles, conversations, and observations of the people I interact with. I have tried to be light in my corner of the world and have failed miserably sometimes. Call me to seek more knowledge of you so I will cast a reflection of the *true light*. As a new year approaches, work in me, Lord Jesus. Let my light "shine before others" so they will see good works in my life and give glory to the Father in heaven (Matt. 5:16). That's how I need to respond to Christmas.

▰ December 28

"He saved us, not because of any works of righteousness that we had done, but according to his mercy . . . [his] Spirit he poured out on us richly through Jesus Christ our Savior, so that, having been justified by his grace, we might become heirs according to the hope of eternal life" (Titus 3:5–7). Father, I can hardly grasp the privilege of being your child! Scripture clearly establishes that you have given me adoption and an inheritance of eternal life. I need constant awareness of this family tie and this sure inheritance, because so much around me breeds disconnectedness, destruction, and despair. Thoughts of "the goodness and loving kindness of God our Savior" (Titus 3:4) are what I need. Give me these thoughts as my refuge and my hope.

■ December 29

Heavenly Father, receiving your kingdom as a little child begins as simply as deciding to accept it with wide eyes and open arms. But if I have taken my adoption into your family for granted, basking in blessings without contributing to the work of the kingdom, forgive me. A child in your family has responsibilities, just as a child in my home is expected to help with chores. And if I have gone the opposite route, burning myself out with too much "kingdom work," remind me that there are no Superwomen in the church—just able women you equip to serve under a reasonable number of hats at one time.

■ December 30

"When I was a child," wrote Paul, "I spoke like a child, I thought like a child, I reasoned like a child; when I became an adult, I put an end to childish ways" (1 Cor. 13:11). Childish ways? That steps on my toes, Lord. I choose to spend many hours on a favorite computer game, ignoring the clutter and undone projects around the house. I reason like a child, even though I am "grown up." I hold stubbornly to what I want to believe, especially about "right" and "wrong," rather than facing the truth as you have spelled it out. Lord, bless me with the surrender I cannot muster on my own, the surrender of my childish ways.

■ December 31

Precious and loving Savior, as another year concludes I continue to be amazed at how fast time passes, as if I am literally over the hill of a roller coaster, speeding downward. I am thankful that you are still out in front, preparing the way for me to pass through life, not just surviving, but finding pleasure and peace. I am depending on you for this, Lord. Thank you for being dependable when everything else (including me) is changing. Give me the ability to approach life with both the enthusiasm of childhood and the wisdom of adulthood. In the coming year, continue to transform me from the self-made Superwoman I have tried to be into the Spirit-made woman you are calling me to be.

topical index

Scripture
    applying Scripture to life Jan. 6, Mar. 24, June 30,
        Nov. 8
    learning Scripture Sept. 7
    relying on Scripture Sept. 18
    trustworthiness of Scripture Mar. 10, June 22, July 27
    understanding Scripture Sept. 26, Nov. 8
security Mar. 31, Sept. 12, Oct. 30
self-denial Jan. 21, Mar. 17, July 8
self-esteem/self-worth. *See* personal value
self-reliance/self-sufficiency July 5
selfishness Nov. 26
sensitivity Sept. 9
silence Sept. 14
sin May 1, 17, Aug. 6
speech Jan. 8, Apr. 7, May 24, 25, Aug. 22, Sept. 20, Nov. 17,
        Dec. 7, 12, 13
spiritual adoption Dec. 28, 29
spiritual discipline Mar. 3, May 18, July 23
spiritual freedom July 1, 3, 4, 14
spiritual fruitfulness July 24
spiritual maturity Mar. 18, Dec. 30
spiritual nourishment Jan. 27, Mar. 28, Apr. 28, Oct. 9,
        Nov. 10
spiritual warfare Mar. 8, Apr. 27, May 22–27
stewardship May 29, July 10
stress Aug. 2, 3
strength Aug. 3

television June 18, Aug. 25
temptation Aug. 6
thankfulness Jan. 15, Apr. 2, Nov. 19, 24
time/time management Jan. 23, Mar. 17, Apr. 4, 5, 20, 21,
        June 29, Sept. 19
tolerance Nov. 21
transformation July 22, 23, 25, Dec. 31